The purpose of this study guide is to provide supplemental educational material. It is not intended as a substitute or replacement of THE HEART OF REDNESS.

Published by SuperSummary, www.supersummary.com

ISBN – 9781074306120

For more information or to learn about our complete library of study guides, please visit http://www.supersummary.com

Please submit any comments, corrections, or questions to: http://www.supersummary.com/support/

TABLE OF CONTENTS

PLOT OVERVIEW

South African novelist Zakes Mda published his satirical work *The Heart of Redness* in 2000. In the novel, Mda blends history, myth, and realist fiction to portray a South African village over a 150-year span. In 1856, a 15-year-old girl from kwaXhosa named Nongqawuse told her uncle, Mhlakaza, that she had encountered the spirits of two of her ancestors. These spirits told the young girl that if the amaXhosa killed all their cattle, destroyed their crops, and abandoned witchcraft, then the dead would be resurrected, and the white invaders would be swept into the sea. The resulting famine from the cattle-killing and crop destruction caused approximately 80,000 deaths and was used by the British to consolidate their control over the land.

Twin and Twin-Twin are two brothers who fall on either side of the cattle-killing prophesies. While Twin believes in the prophesies and participates in the destruction, his brother Twin-Twin denounces Nongqawuse, and is eventually forced into aligning himself with the British government in order to protect his homestead, family, and cattle from his brother and the other "Believers." Disgusted by all forms of religion, Twin-Twin eventually starts his own cult of "Unbelievers."

The actions of their ancestors have profound effects on the progeny of both Twin and Twin-Twin. The feud continues into the 21st century and post-apartheid South Africa. Bhonco, Twin-Twin's direct descendant, has inherited the scars that Twin-Twin suffered after being accused of being a wizard. He has resurrected the cult of the Unbelievers and continues to feud with the descendants of Twin. Zim, the direct descendant of Twin, continues in the faith of his ancestor and has passed his strong belief in the prophesies to his daughter, Qukezwa.

Camagu spent most of his life in the United States but returned to South Africa to rebuild his country after the fall of apartheid. But in Johannesburg, Camagu finds that his country does not want his help, and so plans to go back into "exile." Instead of driving to the airport, Camagu takes a 10-hour detour to Qolorha-by-Sea to see if he can find the woman who had captivated him the night before. While he does not find her, he finds two other women who appeal to different sides of him. One is Xoliswa Ximiya, the beautiful and accomplished daughter of Bhonco. As the headmistress of the local secondary school, Xoliswa Ximiya rejects tradition and wants to see her country develop along the lines of the United States. The other appealing woman is Zim's daughter, Qukezwa. She is different from Xoliswa Ximiya in every way. She reveres the past and feels connected to the land in a way that Xoliswa Ximiya never will. The soul of the village is played out in this struggle over Camagu's soul as he reconnects with the part of himself that has been in exile over all these years.

CHAPTER SUMMARIES AND ANALYSES

Chapters 1-3

Chapter 1 Summary

Post-Apartheid South Africa

In the 150 years since Xikixa's death and decapitation at the hands of the British, his descendants have splintered into two camps, the "Believers" and the "Unbelievers." Chapter 1 introduces us to Bhonco, who "resurrected the cult" (6) of Unbelievers. Bhonco is a man easily moved to tears by the beauty in the world. He is happily married to NoPetticoat, and although the "custom is that men walk in front and women follow" (4), they walk side by side, sometimes holding hands. Their public displays of affection are a source of embarrassment to their daughter, Xoliswa Ximiya, an educated, successful, and unmarried educator, who feels that "old people have no right to love" (4). Xoliswa Ximiya informs her parents that she has no intention of accepting the promotion to principal of Qolorha-by-Sea Secondary School. Instead, she wants to "work for the Ministry of Education in Pretoria, or at the very least in Bisho" (12). The parents are dead set against her living so far away from them, and NoPetticoat blames her husband, telling him, "You see, Bhonco, you should never have allowed this child to take that scholarship to America" (12).

The Middle Generations

Xikixa, Bhonco's great-great-grandfather, was an aristocrat in the time of King Sarhili:

He was the father of the twins, Twin and Twin-Twin. Twin-Twin was the first of the twins to be born, so according to custom he was the younger. The older one is the one who is the last to kick the doors of the womb and to breathe the air that has already been breathed by the younger brother (13).

In the beginning, "Twin and Twin-Twin were like one person" (13), so much so that their father was relieved when they finally "took up sticks" (15) against each other. They fought over whether Mlanjeni was the resurrection of the Prophet Nxele, as thought by Twin, or whether he was a "prophet in his own right" (15) as argued by Twin-Twin. Xikixa tells his sons, "I was becoming worried about you two […] Now you are becoming human beings" (15).

This would not be the only time that the issue of Mlanjeni's divinity divided the twins. Two poles were resurrected by Mlanjeni and his followers, and while "the clean" walked between them "unscathed," the "unclean were struck by weakness and fear as they approached the poles" and then they "writhed on the spot, unable to move" (16). This is how the witches and wizards were identified. When Twin-Twin's senior wife becomes transfixed between the poles, she is declared a witch. Because Twin-Twin defends her, he is denounced as a wizard, dragged away, and whipped. Instead of blaming Mlanjeni, both his father and brother blame Twin-Twin "for stupidly defending the honor of a woman who had been declared a witch by none other than the great prophet himself" (17).

Sir Harry Smith, the self-proclaimed "Great White Chief of the Xhosas" runs "wild all over the lands of the amaXhosa," doing whatever he wants "in the name of Queen Victoria of England" (18), including deposing King Sandile and having the chiefs, including Xikixa, kiss both his staff and his boots. When the British decide to hunt down Mlanjeni, "claiming they did not approve of his witch-hunting and witch-cursing activities" (17), Twin-Twin, though bitter at the treatment that both he and his senior wife suffered on account of the prophet, takes up arms alongside his father, brother, and the other men of kwaXhosa to defend Mlanjeni. During the three years of "The Great War of Mlanjeni" (19), the prophet promises "that the guns of the British would shoot hot water instead of bullets" (19). Preparing to ambush a British camp, the twins and their compatriots watch in horror as the British soldiers decapitate a dead umXhosa soldier and toss the severed head into a pot of boiling water. It is not until after they raid the camp that they realize that the severed head belongs to their father, Xikixa. Before they can torture and kill their father's murderers, including an interpreter named John Dalton, British reinforcements run them off.

In the aftermath, the "Khoikhoi people of the Kat River Valley abandon their traditional alliance with the British and fought on the side of the amaXhosa" (19). To do so, the "Khoikhoi women sold their bodies to the British soldiers in order to smuggle canisters of gunpowder to their fighting men" (21). At first Twin and his friends make disparaging remarks about these women, seeming "to forget that it was for the gunpowder that was saving the amaXhosa nation from utter defeat that the women were prostituting themselves" (21). But when Twin falls in love with Qukezwa, one of these Khoikhoi women who "opened their thighs for British soldiers" (23), he cannot be dissuaded by Twin-Twin, who would rather see his brother marry an amaXhosa maiden.

The long war takes its toll on both sides. Sir Harry Smith is recalled to his country in disgrace" when his soldiers refuse "to go to the Amathole Mountains to be slaughtered like cattle by the savage amaXhosa" (21). Sir Harry Smith is replaced by Sir George Cathcart, who proceeds "to the eastern frontier to attend to the war with great enthusiasm" (21). As for the amaXhosa, they are "disappointed with Mlanjeni's prophesies. None of them were coming true. The Imperial bullets did not turn into water. Instead, amaXhosa men were being killed every day" (21). Because he cannot "defeat the amaXhosa people in the field of battle," Sir George Cathcart starves "them into submission" (24). He orders his soldiers to burn the fields and slaughter the cattle belonging to the amaXhosa people. They also murder "unarmed women working in the fields" (24). The amaXhosa surrender to the British and they turn "against Mlanjeni, the Man of the River, because his charms had failed" (24). Mlanjeni dies of tuberculosis six months after the war ends.

Chapter 2 Summary

Post-Apartheid South Africa

Now in his mid-40s, Camagu had spent almost 30 years in "exile" in America where he completed a doctoral degree and developed his "skills in the area of development communication" (29). He "worked for international agencies" and "as an international expert he had done consulting work for UNESCO in Paris and for the Food and Agricultural Organization in Rome" (29). In 1994, he took leave from his job to return to South Africa and cast his vote in the elections, and "swept up by the euphoria of the time" (29), decided to stay in his home country and lend his skills to the remaking of South Africa. However, those charged with rebuilding South Africa view him as unpatriotic for having deserted his country.

At one interview, he is asked several questions about his familiarity with the country: "You have been out of the country for many years. What makes you think that you can do this job? How familiar are you with South Africa and its problems?" (30). Camagu, whose pride often gets in the way of his achieving success, responds, "How familiar are our rulers, presidents, ministers, and lawmakers—who have either been in prison or in exile for thirty years—with South Africa and its problems?" (30). Camagu could have used his connections in the country to secure a position, but he operates "under the misguided notion that things happened for you because you deserved them, not because you had the most influential lobbyists" (30).

Teaching part-time at a trade school in Johannesburg, Camagu becomes even more disillusioned when his students protest by taking the principal hostage. After a week, the students' demands are met, the principal is released, and the cabinet minister who negotiated the terms praises the students for their victory. There is no accountability for the students or justice for the principal. At that point, "Camagu's hopes that things would come right were crushed" (34), and he resigns from the school, packs his suitcase, and plans to head back to America the next day.

The night before he plans "to go back to exile" (31) Camagu is restless. He lives over a nightclub called Giggles in the neighborhood of Hillbrow. When he tells his fellow club-goers that his bags are packed, they hurl accusations at him, saying that he is unpatriotic because he is "deserting his country in its hour of need for imperialistic America" (27). He wants to walk the streets, but he is "dead scared of this town" (27) and decides to join a funeral procession entering his 20-story building. While there, he becomes captivated by a beautiful woman singing hymns for the dead. Afterwards, Camagu speaks to the woman and finds out that her name is NomaRussia and she lives in Qolorha-by-Sea. She had come to Hillbrow to "visit her 'homeboy,' only to find" (35) that he is dead.

Chapter 3 Summary

Post-Apartheid South Africa

While Bhonco, a direct descendant of Twin-Twin, "resurrected the cult" (6) of Unbelievers, Zim, a direct descendant of Twin, is "the leading light of the Believers" (36). He even named his son and daughter after his ancestors, Twin and Qukezwa. Still mourning the death of his wife, NoEngland, a year earlier, Zim finds solace under his wild fig tree, for "it knows all his secrets. It is his confessional" (38). It also offers a direct link to his ancestor, having been planted by Twin, and "spreading wide like an umbrella over his whole homestead" (38).

Qukezwa disrupts her father's meditations by shouting angrily at him: "You see the disgraceful things you do, tata? Now people shout at me at work! Do you want me to lose my job?" (39). Qukezwa works at Vulindlela Trading Store, owned by John Dalton, the direct descendent of the interpreter who took part in the desecration of Xikixa's corpse. While Dalton's wife is "a Free State Afrikaner" who has never bothered to learn isiXhosa, they say of John Dalton, that though "his skin is white like the skins of those who caused the sufferings of the Middle Generations […] his heart is an umXhosa heart" (8).

That day at work, a group of young women shouts at Qukezwa: "Your mother was a filthy woman! She must be rotting in hell for what she did to that poor girl" (39). Missis Dalton threw the young women out but told

Qukezwa that if she brought fights into the store, she would ask Mr. Dalton to fire her.

Two years prior, Qukezwa's mother, NoEngland, had taken on an assistant to help her sew school uniforms. The two women became close, but the young girl set her sights on Zim. Flattered by the young girl's interest in him, Zim gave way to temptation and had a secret affair with the young girl: "But the girl became too greedy and selfish. She was not satisfied with the occasional tryst. She wanted Zim for herself alone." (40). The young woman went to a famous diviner, or *igqirha*, to help her steal Zim away from NoEngland. The diviner told the young girl to bring one of NoEngland's undergarments to him and he would "'work it" (40) and Zim would love only the girl. But when the young woman brought one of NoEngland's petticoats to the diviner, he recognized it as belonging to Zim's wife. He brought it to NoEngland and let her in on the young woman's plans. He then told NoEngland to bring him one of the young woman's undergarments, which she did. He "worked it" (41) and since "that day the girl has never been able to have another tryst with anyone. Lovers have run away from her because whenever she tries to know a man—in the biblical sense, that is," her period comes "in gushes, like water from a stream" (41). In defending himself, Zim tells his daughter, "We are not supposed to talk ill of the dead, but your mother was not so innocent in this matter [...] How do you think the igqirha knew that was her petticoat?" (41).

Qukezwa talks to her father about moving to Johannesburg and becoming a clerk. Her brother Twin, a successful artist, had left Qolorha-by-Sea after suffering a broken heart. He had been in love with Bhonco's daughter for many years, but Xoliswa Ximiya eventually "outgrew Twin as she became more educated. [...] Villagers, however, still hope to this day that the two will eventually marry and bring about peace between the two families" (43).

The next day was "nkamnkam day," when pensioners receive their checks and get them cashed at the Vulindlela Trading Store. John Dalton deducts any amount they owe on credit, or *ityala*, and if there is cash left over, he gives it to the pensioner: "For those who have been careless during the month there will be no money. The whole pension check will be swallowed up by their ityala. The next month the vicious cycle of debt will continue" (45). For some unexplained reason, Bhonco is the only elder who does not receive his pension, a fact that Zim throws in the Unbeliever's face.

The Middle Generations

The cattle of the amaXhosa people are dying in droves. Lungsickness, a disease "brought to the land of the amaXhosa nation by Friesland bulls that came in a Dutch ship two years earlier, in 1853" (50), is decimating the herds, and "the maize in the fields was attacked by a disease that left it whimpering and blighted" (51). In an effort to protect their cattle, the twins and their families relocate to Qolorha.

In their new home they are reintroduced to Mhlakaza. When they had known him before, he had gone by the name of Wilhelm Goliath:

> At first he was baptized in the Methodist Church, and married his wife, Sarah, from the clan of the amaMfengu, in that church. But soon enough he deserted his Methodist friends and threw in his lot with the Anglicans. The Methodists, he said, told their hearts in public. He preferred the private confessions of the

Anglicans. Also, the Anglicans wore more beautiful robes. (48).

The twins did not treat Wilhelm Goliath seriously. Twin-Twin asks, "This man is from such a distinguished family. His father was King Sarhili's councillor. What is he doing with these people who were cast into the sea?" (49). He is referring to the white people who led the Methodist and Anglican churches. But while the twins agree on the ridiculousness of Wilhelm Goliath, they still disagree on Mlanjeni. Twin-Twin blames Mlanjeni for their father's death, while Twin still considers him to be a "true prophet" (50).

Mhlakaza, who no longer answers to Wilhelm Goliath, explains that once the Anglicans settled, he was treated more like a servant than a holy man in his own right. He left and returned to his ancestral home. Now he calls a public meeting to tell the people of Qolorha that his niece, Nongqawuse, and his sister-in-law, Nombanda, have had a vision. They had been given a message that the "existing cattle are rotten and unclean. They have been bewitched. They must all be destroyed" (54).

Post-Apartheid South Africa

On his way to the airport to catch his flight to America, Camagu impulsively decides to make the 10-hour drive to Qolorha-by-Sea. After waiting in line behind the pensioners at Vulindlela Trading Store, Camagu asks to speak to the owner and his wife. The salesperson instructs Qukezwa to take Camagu to the Daltons' home. On the short walk over, Qukezwa informs Camagu that she is single and offers herself up to him. Camagu is taken aback by the young girl's forwardness.

John Dalton does not know the NomaRussia that Camagu is looking for, but he is "fascinated by an umXhosa man who has spent so many years living in America" (57). After a two-hour talk, Camagu decides to stay the night at the Blue Flamingo Hotel.

Chapters 1-3 Analysis

For the amaXhosa, the past is not the past. Rather than treating each new life as a clean slate, the impact of prior generations is keenly felt. In the first and third chapters Mda navigates between present-day passages and those from the "Middle Generations" (4). Rather than using a linear approach, Mda shows events from different centuries to be happening simultaneously, as if in parallel universes. However, these timelines do not exist entirely separate from one another. Even though Twin-Twin is Bhonco's great-grandfather, they have a present-day relationship:

> Twin-Twin was a naughty man. Even after he died he became a naughty ancestor. Often he showed himself naked to groups of women gathering wood on the hillside or washing clothes in a stream. He was like that in life too. [...] Bhonco carries the scars that were inflicted on his great-grandfather, Twin-Twin, by men who flogged him after he had been identified as a wizard by Prophet Mlanjeni, the Man of the River. Every first boy-child in subsequent generations of Twin-Twin's tree is born with the scars. Even those of the Middle Generations, their first males carried the scars (13).

It is only the second chapter that seems stuck in the late 1990's. Camagu's existence in Johannesburg seems bereft of spirituality and connection to the past: "Camagu used to see himself as a pedlar of dreams. That was when he could make things happen. Now he has lost his touch. He needs a pedlar of dreams himself, with a bagful of dreams waiting to be dreamt" (36). It is not until he is lured to Qolorha-by-Sea by the phantom-like NomaRussia that he is able to reestablish his connection to the past.

The third chapter returns to Qolorha-by-Sea. Although divided into two camps, both the Believers and the Unbelievers are visited by the past. After "Zim assures his daughter that if she works hard enough she will end up being a prophetess like Nongqawuse. […] Qukezwa dreams of Nongqawuse flying with a crow—the Nomyayi bird" (47). Qukezwa makes sure that she sleeps "with her legs stretched out. She will, therefore, be able to run away from her dreams if they become nightmares" (47).

Chapters 4-6

Chapter 4 Summary

Post-Apartheid South Africa

In Qolorha-by-Sea, "Camagu is filled with a searing longing for an imagined blissfulness of his youth" (59). His family left their ancestral village when he was a toddler "to settle in the township of Orlando East, in the city of Johannesburg" (59). Shortly after arriving in the village, he finds himself at a gathering thrown by Bhonco, to celebrate his daughter's promotion to school principal. Bhonco welcomes him and sends Camagu inside the house so that this educated man can sit with the rest of the teachers. The Believers have boycotted the festivities, just as the Unbelievers refuse to attend feasts thrown by the Believers. The teachers at the table comment on this, asking, "How far can you stretch pettiness?" (62).

When asked what brings him to Qolorha-by-Sea, Camagu repeats a story he has concocted to find the woman with whom he has become obsessed. He tells the teachers the story:

> [There was] a young woman called NomaRussia from these parts who worked for him in Johannesburg. He released her from work because he was going to the United States to live there. Only when he was on the way to the airport did he discover that NomaRussia had inadvertently taken his passport with her (63).

Even though he doesn't make any headway in finding NomaRussia, he has trouble keeping his eyes off Bhonco's daughter, Xoliswa Ximiya: "He does not remember seeing anyone quite so beautiful before [...] it is the kind of beauty that is cold and distant, though" (64). When Xoliswa Ximiya hears that Camagu is headed to the United States, she assumes that he has never been there before and describes the wonders of America in detail: "Her colleagues are beginning to fidget. Obviously they have been subjected to this harangue before" (65). When he finally explains that he had spent most of his life in the United States, Xoliswa Ximiya becomes angry that he has embarrassed her in front of her colleagues. She decides to ignore him, but she is drawn back in when she realizes that her friend, Vathiswa, is gaining Camagu's attention. Eventually, a fight breaks out among two of the male teachers, and Xoliswa Ximiya leads Camagu away from the melee. They make arrangements to meet the next day.

As Camagu goes to leave the gathering, Bhonco joins him and lays out the main present-day conflict between the Believers and the Unbelievers. The Believers are "bent on opposing everything that is meant to improve the lives of the people of Qolorha" (70). In contrast, "[t]he Unbelievers are moving forward with the times. That is why they support the casino and the water-sports paradise that the developers want to build. The Unbelievers stand for civilization" (71). Camagu leaves the festivities confused about why the Believers would want to stand in the way of progress.

The next day, not realizing that Xoliswa Ximiya does not live with her parents, Camagu accidentally crashes a meeting that the Unbelievers are holding at Bhonco's home. He is invited to join them, and he watches as the elders dance, sing, and "talk in tongues" (73). Although he sees this unusual behavior, he knows the meaning of what they do:

> But they are not talking in tongues the way that Christians do. They are going into a trance that takes them back to the past. To the world of the ancestors. Not the Otherworld where the ancestors live today. Not the world that lives parallel to our world. But to the world when it still belonged to them (73).

The Middle Generations

Lungsickness has followed the twins to their new home. When the disease takes his prize horse, Gxagxa, Twin starts to wane away himself. It is not until he finds solace in Nongqawuse's prophesies that he finds meaning in life again. But Twin-Twin tries to talk his brother out of following the prophetess:

> 'Don't you see, all the words she utters are really Mhlakaza's words? She is Mhlakaza's medium. The same Mhlakaza who was spreading lies, telling us that we must follow the god of the white man. The very white man who killed the son of his own god!' (76).

Twin-Twin is unable to sway his brother:

> Twin was attracted not only by the good news that new cattle would come with the new people from the Otherworld. Nongqawuse had also pronounced that if the people killed all their cattle and set all their granaries alight, the spirits would rise from the dead and drive all the white people into the sea (77).

The two brothers drift further and further apart in their beliefs. Twin makes one last attempt to convince his brother to accept Nongqawuse's prophesies. When he gets to Twin-Twin's home, he interrupts a meeting of the Unbelievers, who are strategizing ways to convince King Sarhili that Nongqawuse is a false prophetess. Twin is surprised to see his brother in the company of people like "Ned and Mjuza, who were descendants of amaXhosa heroes but were now followers of white ways" (85). Mjuza was even "sometimes seen in the company of John Dalton" (86), one of the men who took part in their father's decapitation. For his part, Twin-Twin is also uncomfortable that he has been forced "to form a strange alliance with people who had deserted their own god for the god of the white man" (85).

Post-Apartheid South Africa

Camagu tries to tell Xoliswa Ximiya about "the memory ritual of the Unbelievers" and the "graceful pain that captivated him" (87). The young principal lets him know that she finds the elders' connection to the past embarrassing. Later, walking through Nongqawuse's Valley, Camagu encounters Qukezwa riding bareback on her horse, Gxagxa. She teases Camagu about his NomaRussia, and he begs her to tell him where he can find the mysterious woman. Instead, Qukezwa gives Camagu a lesson. When he criticizes her for needlessly destroying plants, she asks him:

'Nice plants, eh? Nice for you, maybe. But not nice for indigenous plants. This is the inkberry. It comes from across the Kei River. It kills other plants. These flowers that you like so much will eventually become berries. Each berry is a prospective plant that will kill the plants of my forefathers. And this plant is poisonous to animals too, although its berries are not. Birds eat the berries without any harm, and spread these terrible plants with their droppings' (90).

Chapter 5 Summary

Post-Apartheid South Africa

At a public meeting where the topic of development is discussed, "it is difficult for many people to know which side to take. Even Camagu, with all his learning, cannot make up his mind" (91). He has been visiting with Xoliswa Ximiya every day and has heard Bhonco's opinions on the matter, but he is still not convinced that development is the answer. At the meeting, Zim teases Bhonco for having only one structure on his land and the one he does have for being the old-fashioned rondavel instead of a modern hexagon. It is seen as bad form to attack a man for his lack of possessions. When Camagu takes leave of Xoliswa Ximiya he gives her a kiss on the cheek. The villagers take notice. They are counting on Camagu to save Xoliswa Ximiya from dying an old maid.

The next morning, Camagu is in the shower when he hears the maid scream. It turns out that she discovered a Majola in his bed. Camagu saves the snake from being killed. The Majola is the totem of Camagu's people, the amaMpondomise clan. Exited by the honor of being visited by the snake, Camagu leaves the Majola in his bed and takes a walk down to the lagoon, where he sees Qukezwa emerging from the water. They argue about his "girlfriend," Xoliswa Ximiya. Playing on the visit from his totem, Qukezwa calls her former teacher a snake. She accuses the new headmistress of valuing beauty over everything else. It is a characterization that Camagu cannot easily dismiss. He decides that it is safer not to be enemies with Qukezwa and tries to get her on his side.

Camagu ends up following Qukezwa to Nongqawuse's Valley, and they argue again about Xoliswa Ximiya. Qukezwa accuses Camagu's "girlfriend" of not believing in the ancestors: "Just like all of you whose heads have been damaged by white man's education" (104). Camagu takes offense at this since he does believe in the ancestors. He then listens as Qukezwa talks of the Middle Generations:

> We stood here and saw the wonders. The whole ridge was covered with people who came to see the wonders. [...] Camagu is seized by a bout of madness. He fights hard against the urge to hold this girl, tightly, and kiss her all over. It is different from the urge he once had: to hold and protect Xoliswa Ximiya. This woman does not need protecting. He does (105).

The Middle Generations

Nongqawuse tells her followers that the new people and new cattle will not rise as long as the Unbelievers refuse to kill their cattle and destroy their crops. This puts even more stress on the relationship between the twins. Accused of being disloyal because his brother is one of the leading Unbelievers, Twin proves his commitment to the prophets by leading two attacks on his brother's homestead. In the first, the Believers destroy Twin-Twin's cattle and crops. In the second, they light his homes on fire:

> [Twin-Twin] was running from hut to hut, making sure that all his children were safe, when he came face-to-face with his brother, leading the men who were now singing triumphantly and dancing around the burning homestead (112).

Unbelievers like Twin-Twin find refuge in the mountains. He and his family are forced to become beggars, except for his main wife, who has left him for the Believers. The scars on his back begin to itch, as they begin to itch for his descendant, Bhonco, as well.

Post-Apartheid South Africa

Bhonco is ambivalent to the talk of an impending wedding between his daughter and Camagu. The alliance would afford him greater stature in the village, but he might lose his daughter to one of the big cities, or even to the United States.

Camagu goes to Vulindlela Trading Store, hoping to catch a glimpse of Qukezwa. Instead he meets up with John Dalton, and the businessman explains why he has aligned himself with the Believers when it comes to trying to stop the new business developments. Camagu understands that instead of creating wealth for the villagers, "it will take all the little money that there is in the village" (117). Since Camagu wants to stay in the village longer, John Dalton offers to try and set him up as a caretaker for one of the vacation cottages. They head over to Zim's house to give him the news that Camagu is staying on in Qolorha-by-Sea, and that he is also against development.

Zim is distrustful of Camagu. He has heard that the younger man will soon marry Xoliswa Ximiya, making him Bhonco's son-in-law:

> 'I am not anyone's son-in-law,' says Camagu, beginning to lose his patience. 'And I am not an Unbeliever. I am not a Believer either. I don't want to be dragged into your quarrels. My ancestors were not even here among yours when the beginning of your bad blood happened' (118).

Camagu suggests that their side just can't stand against development. They have to have a plan in place to help the people of Qolorha-by-Sea prosper without the casinos and water-sports schemes. In the middle of their meeting Qukezwa comes home. When Zim introduces her to Camagu, she pretends that they have never met.

The next day, Camagu encounters Qukezwa at the lagoon and confronts her: "He grabs her arm and demands, 'Why did you pretend you didn't know me?'" (120). Rather than answering his question, she teases him about the effects that the oysters she served him in her father's house had on him. She then tells him a story about how she used to be scared of the sea. Her mother never let her go to the sea by herself. Once, she snuck away with a friend and almost drowned. That night her mother beat her for going into the sea alone: "Since her mother's death she has learned how to swim, and has become quite an expert at harvesting the sea. Now she swims with a vengeance and is not scared of the most vicious storms" (121).

Chapter 6 Summary

The Middle Generations

Even though Twin-Twin has aligned himself with John
Dalton when it comes to the cattle-killing issue, he has not
forgotten the part that Dalton played in his father's death.
For his part, the white interpreter does not trust Twin-Twin:

> [Dalton] was not happy when Ned and Mjuza suggested
> that [Twin-Twin] should be saved from his mountain
> refuge and set up in a new homestead in Qolorha, near
> Chief Nxito's deserted Great Place, where he would
> receive protection from the marauding bands of
> Believers. Dalton had to go along with the idea because
> it was important to show the natives—especially those
> that were heathens like Twin-Twin—that people who
> were on the side of the British Empire would receive full
> protection (124).

Unlike the others, Twin-Twin complains to Dalton that the
British are taking land away from the amaXhosa. He is
unwilling to accept that receiving "British civilization"
(123) in return is a good trade-off.

John Dalton prepares the elders for a meeting with Sir
George Grey, the new governor of the Cape Colony since
the last governor, Sir George Cathcart, died. Sir George
Grey has been given the derisive nickname of "The Man
Who Named Ten Rivers" (84) by the amaXhosa, after he
went about naming rivers and mountains that already had
names. Although Sir George Grey does not require any
boot-kissing, he does make it clear "that the chiefs had no
option but to accept" (125) the British government's new
administrative system. When Grey complains that the
amaXhosa still seek out their own traditional doctors, the

chiefs explain that it is because the "amaXhosa doctors are also spiritual healers" (127). The governor contends that this practice is outdated:

> 'That is precisely what we must change,' said the governor. 'We must get rid of all these superstitions. That is what civilization will do for you. That is another matter I have been discussing with the chiefs. You see, I plan to open a school in Cape Town for the sons of chiefs, where they will grow up in the bosom of civilization. They will learn to appreciate the might of the British Empire and will acquire new modes of behavior. They will give up their barbaric culture and heathen habits, and when they take over in their chiefdoms they will be good chiefs. I want all the chiefs to undertake to send their sons to this school' (127).

Although Twin gets more fervent in his beliefs, the rift in his relationship with his brother troubles him. He blames the state of their relationship on the fact that their father had been decapitated: "Without a head Xikixa was unable to bring cohesion to his progeny. That was why they were fighting among themselves, and were destined to do so until his headless state was remedied" (129). Twin believes that reconciliation will only be possible when the new people and cattle are resurrected, and when the white man is pushed back into the sea.

The prophetesses set the date of the resurrection for the "full moon of June 1856" (129), but when the ancestors do not arrive from the Otherworld, some followers stop believing in the resurrection. This becomes known as the "First Disappointment." The prophetesses then set another date in mid-August, and when again, the ancestors do not come, this becomes known as the "Second Disappointment." When King Sarhili summons Mhlakaza to explain himself, Mhlakaza "denied that he was the source of the prophesies. He put all the blame on Nongqawuse. 'She is the one who talks with the new people,' he said. 'I am merely her mouth'" (131). Eventually, he satisfies the king by explaining that the new people did not come because some Believers sold their cattle instead of slaughtering them, and some did not carry out the ritual satisfactorily when slaughtering their cattle.

Twin-Twin is increasingly more troubled as the Unbelievers' collaboration with the British deepens. When it becomes known that the British are going to put the chiefs on the government payroll, and they will no longer have to decide on legal cases, it is Twin-Twin who recognizes this as a power grab:

> 'The white man does not know our law,' said Twin-Twin vehemently. 'He does not respect our law. He will apply the law of the English people. This is a way of introducing his laws among our people. As for the colonial money, The Man Who Named Ten Rivers is buying our chiefs. When they are paid by him, they will owe their loyalty to him, and not to the amaXhosa people, and not to our laws and customs and traditions!' (134).

Post-Apartheid South Africa

Camagu has started harvesting seafood in order to make a living. Qukezwa, in one of her more magnanimous moods, spends a morning teaching Camagu "the art of catching mussels and oysters, or imbhaza and imbhatyisa" (138). Instead of going into competition with the local women who sell their catch to the Blue Flamingo Hotel and to other villagers, he goes into business with them and drives their combined catch to other towns.

John Dalton meets with some of his British friends but gets angry at their fickle attitude toward South Africa. While the rest of them are planning to leave the country, he is adamant about staying: "The Afrikaner is more reliable than you chaps. He belongs to the soil. He is of Africa. Even if he is not happy about the present situation he will not go anywhere. He cannot go anywhere" (139). When they point out the Afrikaner's racist wish for a white homeland, he calls out his friends' hypocrisy:

> 'Yes, you prided yourselves as liberals [...] But now you can't face the reality of a black-dominated government. It is clear that while you were shouting against the injustices of the system, secretly you thanked God for the National Party which introduced and preserved that very system for forty-six years' (140).

On his way back to his store, Dalton sees Bhonco, and although he gives him a ride, he has the elder sit in the back of the bakkie—"customs do not die easily" (141). When he finds out that Bhonco is planning to fight a family of tourists that embarrassed his wife, Dalton persuades Bhonco to come with him to the store instead. There they find Zim and Camagu, waiting to speak to Dalton about the possibility of planting some botanical gardens. Dalton and Camagu try to claim neutrality, but the hard feeling between Zim and Bhonco make it impossible not to be dragged into their hostilities. At one point, Camagu looks at the door and sees Qukezwa:

> His mind is no longer on the botanical garden. It is wandering somewhere in the clouds. [...] He excuses himself. He must get away from these surroundings that are haunted by Qukezwa's aura. He must fight the demons that take hold of him at the mere thought of her

smile. He must try and be in control. This wild woman cannot possibly be of any good to him (148-49).

That evening he meets Xoliswa Ximiya, but she walks away from him after they have a disagreement over his belief in the Majola as his clan's totem, saying:

'You are an educated man, Camagu, all the way from America. How do you expect simple peasants to give up their superstitions and join the modern world when they see educated people like you clinging to them?' (150).

As he walks home, "[h]e is startled out of his reverie. A silvery beast stands right in front of him. She is sitting on top of it, all silvery in her smug smile" (151). Camagu eventually allows Qukezwa to pull him up on the horse. Then he realizes that he is aroused. He "takes his mind off his dire situation, and sends it to dwell on Xoliswa Ximiya's icy beauty" (152).

Chapters 4-6 Analysis

Camagu's soul is where the latest battle between the Believers and the Unbelievers is being waged. The differences are even more stark in Qukezwa and Xoliswa Ximiya than they are in Zim and Bhonco. While Bhonco still communes with the ancestors and bears the scars of Twin-Twin's beating, Xoliswa Ximiya rejects all "superstition" and looking toward the past.

For Camagu's part, he is torn between everything learned during his 30-year exile and the memories of his ancestral home. His attraction toward Xoliswa Ximiya is guided by his intellect. She is objectively beautiful. He is impressed with her education and intellect, whereas his attraction toward Qukezwa is visceral. While his mind comes up with excuses not to be with her—she has probably slept with a lot of men and carries sexually transmitted diseases, she is not good for him, she is wild—his body betrays itself every time he is around her. Qukezwa is not just a rejection of the white man's way—she is a strong embrace of custom, generational knowledge, and understanding of the environment. Xoliswa Ximiya has no appreciation for what is at hand but is enthralled with what exists elsewhere—either in another city, or across the ocean. When Qukezwa warns Camagu about the inkberry plant, she explains how it came across the river and will choke the life out of indigenous plants. Her people stood against the white man when he came across the sea to supplant the indigenous people of the kwaXhosa, while Xoliswa Ximiya's ancestors made uneasy alliances with the British usurpers.

Sir George Grey is playing the long game when it comes to subjugating the amaXhosa people. He tells the chief that he is planning on building a school in Cape Town where the sons of the chiefs will be given a British education. This tactic of interrupting a subjugated people's cultural education did not end with the British in kwaXhosa. According to the Smithsonian Institute, starting in the late 1800s, Native American parents were often forced to send their children to government and church-operated Indian boarding schools, in which the children were prevented from speaking their languages, practicing their religion, and learning about their history and culture. Instead, they were taught English, forced to adopt Christianity, and take on new names. The US government prevented Native American parents from transmitting their values, culture, and beliefs to their own children.

Further, by putting the chiefs on the British payroll, Sir George Grey was getting buy-ins from those who carried the most authority in the kwaXhosa. That way, he could mitigate the pushback the British conquerors would receive as they began to usurp more land and take control of existing institutions.

Chapters 7-9

Chapter 7 Summary

The Middle Generations

Twin and Qukezwa sit with their young son, Heitsi, "hoping the sun would turn red, and other suns would emerge from behind the mountains" (153), signs that the resurrection was beginning. But the sun continues to rise "as it had risen in the days of their forefathers" (153). When they hear a war cry, the small family races back to the village. The Man Who Named Ten Rivers has sent a ship full of British sailors, and the HMS Geyser is now entering the mouth of the Gxarha River. AmaXhosa soldiers station themselves along the banks, and Qukezwa marshals the women to bring up the rear and produce "the sharp undulating wails that every umXhosa woman produced so well" (155). As a Khoikhoi woman, Qukezwa has never mastered the art of ululation.

The battle is averted when a group of British sailors nearly drown when they try to disembark the ship. The ship ends up retreating, and the victory over the British Navy emboldens the Believers commitment to the prophesies and cattle-killing.

Alternatively, Twin-Twin becomes convinced that the cattle-killing prophesies were master-minded by The Man Who Named Ten Rivers in an effort to divide the amaXhosa people and steal their land. The Unbelievers who have adopted Christianity disregard Twin-Twin's assertions.

Just as the Unbelievers have a split in their camp, the Believers also splinter when a new prophetess emerges. An 11-year-old girl named Nonkosi also claims to have visions of the Strangers, but, unlike Nongqawuse, Nonkosi encourages her followers to maintain an austere appearance. Instead of choosing between the two prophetesses, Twin and Qukezwa make their home in both camps.

Post-Apartheid South Africa

Camagu has bought a cottage by the sea, and at his housewarming party, Xoliswa Ximiya publicly takes him to task because the cooperative he has started now makes traditional isiXhosa costumes that are sold in Johannesburg. She complains to Camagu: "My people are trying to move away from redness, but you are doing your damnedest to drag them back" (160). To escape Xoliswa Ximiya, Camagu joins the elders on the porch, but he is scolded by his older guests for having running water in his new house while the communal taps have been shut off. Since Dalton is the one who started the communal taps project, and eventually shut it off due to nonpayment by the villagers, Camagu calls Dalton out onto the porch to answer for his own actions. Eventually, Dalton's grandfather's role as a "headhunter" (168) is thrown in his face, and the tensions continue to escalate.

The next day, Camagu goes to Zim's homestead looking for Qukezwa. Camagu convinces her to meet him at the lagoon. When she finally arrives, he begs her for another "ride on Gxagxa [...] like the other night," (172). Qukezwa turns him down and gallops away. Camagu watches as she is stopped by the friends of the "poor girl" who became cursed when she tried to steal Zim away from NoEngland. They accuse Qukezwa of running around with Xoliswa Ximiya's boyfriend. Qukezwa replies that their "friend is the whore in this whole matter" (173), and then she precedes to charge the girls on horseback, injuring one of them.

That night, Camagu is eating dinner in his cottage when Xoliswa Ximiya's friend, Vathiswa, comes to fetch the CDs that she had brought to the housewarming party. Camagu invites her in, but Vathiswa is hesitant. She does not want the villagers to think that she has designs on Xoliswa Ximiya's man. Camagu tells her that he does not belong to anyone and convinces her to come inside. As they eat dinner together, Camagu asks about the scene he saw between Qukezwa and the other girls. Vathiswa explains that it has nothing to do with him. She tells him the story of Zim's unfaithfulness and the subsequent curse on his young mistress. She then tells Camagu that Qukezwa is pregnant. He responds cynically when Vathiswa explains that the village grandmothers who examined her say she is still a virgin: "Camagu cannot understand why he is filled with anger and bitterness. He remembers the silvery night when she sang him to an orgasm" (174).

Chapter 8 Summary

Post-Apartheid South Africa

The whole village is getting ready for the end of the school year concert. Students are practicing their dances, while workers at the Blue Flamingo Hotel practice their songs. However, while the rest of the villagers focus on the upcoming celebration, Bhonco, Zim, Camagu and Dalton are preoccupied with their own thoughts.

Bhonco is bitter that NoPetticoat is spending all her evenings practicing for the concert. Zim stands on the hill waiting for the Russian ships that the Believers of the Middle Generations waited for during the time of the prophecies. Because it was the Russians that killed Sir George Cathcart during the Crimean War, the Believers regarded the Russians as the spirits of amaXhosa soldiers coming to liberate their people. Camagu tries to keep his thoughts on NomaRussia, but he is increasingly drawn to Qukezwa. Dalton is defensive about his communal water project and cannot understand why the other villagers expect him to keep the taps going when they are unwilling to pay for it. Camagu criticizes Dalton, which has a detrimental effect on their relationship: "You went about this whole thing the wrong way, John. The water project is failing because it was imposed on the people. No one bothered to find out their needs" (179).

The Middle Generations

Twin-Twin continues to rebuff the attempts of his fellow Unbelievers to convert him to Christianity, while Twin and Qukezwa continue to wait for the resurrection. When the prophesy fails to materialize again, Mhlakaza says that the prophetesses "say that the dead will not rise as long as Chief Nxito remains in exile" (185). Chief Nxito, a staunch Unbeliever whose son had ousted him, does believe in the prophesies. Now the prophetesses are saying that Chief Nxito must be returned to power in order for the prophesies to manifest. Twin-Twin thinks that it is a mistake for Chief Nxito to return because it will diminish his authority if he allows himself to be ordered around by young girls. Chief Nxito finally bows to pressure and returns to Qolorha. While he remains an Unbeliever, the rumors start flying that he has been converted by Mhlakaza and the prophetesses.

Bhonco and his fellow Unbelievers engage in a trance that takes them back in time to the Middle Generations. It is a dance that they had borrowed from the abaThwa since the Unbelievers do not have their own dance that can transport them back in time. But when Bhonco returns to consciousness, he realizes that "they are all surrounded by a group of abaThwa, the small people who were called Bushmen by the colonists of old" (187). The abaThwa want their dance back.

On his way to the concert that night, Bhonco plans to have it out with Zim. He believes that it was Zim who put the abaThwa up to taking back their dance from the Unbelievers. He sees Zim seated next to Camagu and sneers at him. At the concert people can pay money to dictate who goes on stage and what they do. At first, the acts go on as expected—the dancers and then the choirs. Eventually, the concertgoers start using the ability to control others through money to escalate their rivalries. Qukezwa invites all the women in the village with the name NomaRussia to come onto the stage. Camagu searches their faces, not finding the NomaRussia that brought him to Qolorha-by-Sea. Then the friends of Zim's mistress pay to have Qukezwa stand on the stage and explain their friend's pain. Qukezwa responds, stating: "Well, the explanation is a very simple one. Their friend caused the pain on herself" (193). John Dalton then pays for Qukezwa to sing in her "split-tone manner" (193). As she does, he admires her:

> Qukezwa sings in such beautiful colors. Soft colors like the ochre of yellow gullies. Reassuring colors of the earth. Red. Hot colors like blazing fire. Deep blue. Deep green. Colors of the valleys and the ocean. Cool colors

like the rain of summer sliding down a pair of naked bodies (193).

Camagu has the same reaction to Qukezwa at the concert that he did riding with her on Gxagxa. He follows her out of the concert and declares his love for her, to which she retorts: "You know nothing about love, learned man!" (194). Qukezwa spits back at him, before leaving. He has humiliated himself in front of the other villagers.

Back at the concert the tensions continue to rise. Bhonco accuses Zim of sending the abaThwa to take back their dance. In turn, Zim spends his savings and "buys" Bhonco's wife, forcing NoPetticoat to ululate for the entirety of the concert.

Camagu stays in his cottage for days until Dalton finally convinces him to come out of hiding. Three developers are holding a meeting and Dalton wants Camagu's support as he tries to dissuade the villagers from supporting the new casino and water-sports ventures. At the meeting, one of the developers describes all the improvements that the businesses will bring to Qolorha-by-Sea. Camagu argues that the villagers will not be able to take part in these improvements, and very few of them will find employment in the tourist trade. When the developer asked how he will stop them, Camagu blurts out the first idea that comes to mind—"I will have this village declared a national heritage site" (201).

That evening, impressed with Camagu's efforts to save Qolorha-by-Sea from the developers, Qukezwa shows up at his cottage. The two ride Gxagxa "bareback, reinless and naked" (203).

Chapter 9 Summary

The Middle Generations

Chief Nxito is anxious to prove the prophetesses false by demanding that Mhlakaza "display to the chiefs of the kwaXhosa those new people he was claiming had already risen from the dead" (207). Mhlakaza agrees, but when his men find Twin-Twin hiding in the place where the new people were to show themselves, Mhlakaza claims, "Nxito has insulted the new people!" (207). Once again, the Unbelievers are blamed for the failure of the prophesies to come about. Later, when King Sarhili goes to the mouth of the Gxarha River, he finds "that Mhlakaza and Nongqawuse had vanished. They had left a message that the new people had angrily returned to the Otherworld because of the despicable behavior of the unbelieving chiefs" (209). King Sarhili, "sad and humiliated," tries "to kill himself with his father's spear" (209).

King Sarhili's faith returns before the full moon in February, the new date set for resurrection by Mhlakaza and the prophetesses. John Dalton, who has become a tradesman, makes money off the starving Believers by selling them candles "so they might have some light during the great darkness" (210). When the sun rises in the sky like any other ordinary day, King Sarhili finally loses "all hope. He took the blame upon himself for issuing the imiyolelo, the orders that people should obey the prophets of Gxarha. He told John Dalton, 'I have been deceived'" (211).

Post-Apartheid South Africa

Qukezwa is brought before the court of Chief Xikixa. She is accused of cutting down wattle and lantana trees. The only tree that can be cut down without the permission of the chief is the mimosa tree, or the *umga*. Bhonco tries to get Zim on the hook for Qukezwa's actions. Bhonco argues that Qukezwa is still a minor since she is unmarried, and therefore, her father is responsible for her actions. However, Qukezwa insists on taking accountability for what she has done. Before the elders can make a decision, the court proceedings are interrupted by the news that a homestead is on fire. Everyone rushes to help put out the fire.

The fire had started at NoGiant's house when her husband, angry that NoGiant asked him to take a bath before he could engage in his "conjugal rights," poured "paraffin all over the rondavel while ranting and raving about her unreasonable demand that he should wash his body" (220). He then set "the house ablaze" (220). Camagu blames himself because it was his idea that the women should work from home rather than together at the cottage, to keep them from "gossiping" (219) and to make them more productive. Qukezwa tries to ease his mind: "You should not worry yourself about that [...] Men are insecure when women make more money. It makes women more independent. Men will just have to get used to it" (220). They then go down to the sea and climb aboard a wrecked ship, the *Jacaranda*, that her father believes is a Russian ship that had arrived "more than a century late" (220).

Later that afternoon, Camagu visits Vulindlela Trading Store. There, Dalton's wife lets Camagu know how disappointed she is in his choice. Qukezwa "is a rotten apple, that one [...] Take Xoliswa Ximiya, for instance. Now there's a lady" (222). Meanwhile, Qukezwa gives birth to her son, who she names "Heitsi" after "Heitsi Eibib, the earliest prophet of the Khoikhoi" (23).

Chapters 7-9 Analysis

Those that believe find reasons to believe. For example, instead of questioning the prophetesses when their prophesies fail over and over again, Believers find evidence of the resurrection in the "victory" over the British sailors, who retreat before a battle can ensue. Twin-Twin believes that the British are responsible for the cattle-killing prophesies, and the British land grab that takes place while the amaXhosa fight among themselves confirms his suspicions. Confirmation bias is the tendency for people to interpret new evidence in such a way that it supports their existing beliefs. Both Twin and Twin-Twin experience the failure of the prophesies to come true over and over again, but while Twin-Twin views that as confirmation that those proposing the cattle killing are false prophets, Twin takes it as evidence that the Unbelievers are blocking the prophesies from coming true through their lack of faith.

At first, Camagu resists the idea that his and Qukezwa's nighttime ride could have resulted in her pregnancy, but his desire to be the father allows him to be open to the grandmothers' pronouncement that Qukezwa is still a virgin. Xoliswa Ximiya balks at the idea that Qukezwa didn't get pregnant by sleeping with a man. They both know what they want to believe, and they let the evidence lead them to that foregone conclusion.

Even though John Dalton's family has been in Qolorha-by-Sea for generations, he still has a paternalistic attitude toward his fellow villagers. Instead of letting the people of Qolorha-by-Sea decide what is best for the village, Dalton bypasses the elders and decides for everyone. While both Camagu and Dalton are outsiders in different ways, Camagu seems to have an innate respect for the people in the village, which Dalton lacks. However, Camagu's presence still causes tension. His cooperative is responsible for women gaining more independence, which threatens the men in their lives. Both men believe that they are doing the right thing, but their ideas are not communally decided. Their way of doing things is more in line with an individualistic society that values independence, as opposed to a communal society that values seniority, consensus, and interdependence.

Chapters 10-12

Chapter 10 Summary

Post-Apartheid South Africa

Bhonco has "become estranged" (225) from beautiful things. Along with Camagu and Zim, he blames Zim's daughter, Qukezwa, for stealing Camagu away from Xoliswa Ximiya. When his daughter comes to visit her parents, she announces that after school ends next week she will travel "to Pretoria to make personal applications" (226) for jobs in the city. Xoliswa Ximiya emphatically denies that it is because Camagu broke her heart. NoPetticoat, who had strongly objected to Xoliswa Ximiya leaving Qolorha-by-Sea earlier, now seems at peace with her daughter's decision, even encouraging her to go.

Zim, instead of being interested in all the activity in his homestead that a new baby brings, thinks only of NoEngland. He misses his wife and his preoccupation is so intense that he has stopped eating or engaging with others. He just lies under his tree, with a smile on his face thinking of NoEngland in the Otherworld. Camagu attempts to visit Qukezwa and Heitsi at Zim's homestead, but the relatives turn him away since he is not recognized as the baby's father.

The Middle Generations

Twin-Twin is seen as useful, and so the British protect him from the marauding Believers who attack the homesteads of the Unbelievers. All other Unbelievers have to fend for themselves. The Man Who Named Ten Rivers "made it clear that the military would be sent only if the hordes strayed into white settlements and farms" (231).

When Twin and Qukezwa arrive at Mhlakaza's home, they find that the religious man has died from starvation. Just as Twin begins to lament the man's death, Mjuza arrives. He is now a member of the British police and he has brought a group of men "to arrest Mhlakaza and the girls" (232). Since he only finds Nombanda in the home, he arrests her and her brother Nqula. Eventually, the authorities find and arrest Nongqawuse and Nonkosi, as well. Twin-Twin hopes this will bring an end to the Believers' cattle-killing and marauding.

Post-Apartheid South Africa

Bhonco struggles with "NoPetticoat's defection to Camagu's cooperative society" (234). Not only does he feel betrayed, he misses her company. However, Camagu refuses to take the blame for NoPetticoat's decision to join the cooperative, reasoning: "No one enticed her there. It is for her own good and the good of her family" (235).

When a man wants to marry a woman, it is customary for the man to send his relatives to make inquiries at the home of the woman's family. Since Camagu does not have any relatives in the village, he and Dalton travel to Zim's homestead so that he can start the process of asking for Qukezwa's hand in marriage. The negotiations take several days and seem to be going well, until Dalton gets drunk and calls Zim's relatives "foolish" (244) for following Nongqawuse and killing their cattle. Camagu challenges Dalton, and the two men argue in front of the relatives. Dalton feels betrayed, and Camagu is ashamed of their behavior. Camagu accuses Dalton of trying to "excavate a buried precolonial identity" (248) with his backward-looking tourist ventures instead of recognizing the amaXhosa's present culture. Dalton accuses Camagu of trying to promote his own cooperative society over Dalton's businesses. Camagu is "despondent" (249) that everyone in the village is talking about the rift in his relationship with Dalton.

The only thing that Camagu can look forward to is Qukezwa and Heitsi coming to live with him in his cottage. But a messenger comes to tell Camagu that Qukezwa will not be coming to live with him for the time being. Zim has gone into a comatose state, and Qukezwa will not leave her father. A healer has been brought in to examine Zim, and he says that the old man is caught between two powerful forces—his wife, NoEngland, is pulling him toward the Otherworld, but Qukezwa is trying to keep him in this world.

While the fight for Zim's soul goes on, a beautiful, but very sick woman, is brought to Zim's homestead on a wooden sleigh. Qukezwa reacts harshly when she sees the woman: "What do you want here? Are you not satisfied with what you did to my mother? Have you come to put the final nail in my father's coffin?" (251). This is the "poor girl" that had an affair with Zim. While the young woman believes it is NoEngland's curse that has caused her illness, the doctors in East London have diagnosed her with cervical cancer. The young woman refuses to move from the homestead until Zim dies. She is hoping that he will ask NoEngland to remove the curse when he meets his wife in

the Otherworld. When Camagu comes to visit Qukezwa
and Heitsi, he recognizes the woman immediately—she is
NomaRussia, the woman he had followed to Qolorha-by-
Sea.

Chapter 11 Summary

The Middle Generations

So many people had starved to death that "[c]orpses and
skeletons were a common sight [...] No one had the
strength to bury them" (253). In an effort to keep his son
alive, Twin goes back to raiding, but now he and the other
Believers are starting to steal from the white colonists.
While Twin keeps his faith in the prophets, Qukezwa
insists they take refuge in the land of the amaMfengu. Once
they arrive, they, like many other Believers, are able to
trade their labor for shelter. While Qukezwa is satisfied to
be able to feed her son, Twin finds the work humiliating.
He threatens to leave, entertaining the thought of reuniting
with Twin-Twin. However, Qukezwa knows that Twin-
Twin will never forgive his brother after everything Twin
has done.

Even though Twin continues to receive protection from the
colonial government, he is resentful:

> The Man Who Named Ten Rivers, who had styled
> himself The Great Benefactor of the Non-European
> Peoples of the World, was taking advantage of the
> defenseless amaXhosa and was grabbing more and more
> of their land for white settlement (256).

Additionally, Sir George complains about "indiscriminate
benevolence" (257) and instructs the chief of the
amaMfengu to "expel those amaXhosa who had found

refuge among his people. Twin and Qukezwa were among the thousands of people who were driven out of the land of the amaMfengu" (258). Because Twin is too weak to be picked up by one of the colonial labor officers, "[h]e ended up an inmate of the Kaffir Relief House, and there he lived with people made raving mad by starvation, until he went raving mad himself" (258). Qukezwa and Heitsi are forced to wander from village to village and beg for food.

Twin-Twin, blaming The Man Who Named Ten Rivers for planting the seed for cattle-killing, and blaming the amaXhosa for allowing themselves to be conquered, becomes "disillusioned with all religions. He therefore invented his own Cult of the Unbelievers—elevating unbelieving to the heights of a religion" (259).

Post-Apartheid South Africa

Bhonco is "at the height of misery" (259). The abaThwa won't lend them their dance anymore, and he and his fellow Unbelievers are unsuccessful in creating a dance that will let them travel to the time of the Middle Generations. He is also feeling intense loneliness. NoPetticoat is spending more and more time with the cooperative society as "she has gained a reputation as the best sewer of umbhaco, which are decorations of black strips that are made on isikhakha skirts and on modern shirts that are inspired by the isikhakha tradition" (260).

Xoliswa Ximiya feels betrayed by her mother's defection to the cooperative society: "She had successfully weaned her parents from redness, until NoPetticoat's rebellion" (260). However, Xoliswa Ximiya has other problems. Not only does she have to accept that she will never win Camagu back, but she has to live with the gossip in the village. Many blame Xoliswa Ximiya for her own broken heart.

They say it is payment for when she was "stingy with her love" (262) and drove Zim's son Twin away. Additionally, Xoliswa Ximiya "wakes up one day and finds that the scars of history have erupted on her body" (261). Bhonco and NoPetticoat never had a son. When others tried to convince Bhonco to take a second wife, he refused: "Now here their daughter is getting the scars. 'What else did they expect?' ask the wagging tongues. 'She is a man in a woman's body. That is why no man can tame her'" (262). Xoliswa Ximiya takes a position with the Department of Education in Pretoria. Bhonco has "lost" his wife, his daughter, and the ability to travel back in time.

At Zim's homestead, the battle over his soul continues to be waged between NoEngland and Qukezwa. Meanwhile, NomaRussia insists on staying outside of Zim's door, hoping that he will intervene with NoEngland on her behalf. Camagu finds himself torn between his commitment to Qukezwa and his attachment to NomaRussia. He admits to the young woman, "Yes. I am engaged to Qukezwa. But it is you who brought me here. It is about you that I dreamt. She merely invaded those dreams" (264). Camagu offers to pay for NomaRussia to live the rest of her short life in relative comfort in a hospice, but she refuses: "No, I will sit here […] at this homestead that brought this on me. I will die here. Let my death hang on their necks for the rest of their days" (266).

When Zim refuses to die, the relatives think it may be because he wants to say goodbye to his son, but NomaRussia tells them that Twin is dead. NomaRussia had gone to Johannesburg to ask Twin to appeal to NoEnglands's "sense of mercy" (267) and lift the curse, but he was already dead. It was at his wake that Camagu first heard NomaRussia singing. When Twin started making wooden carvings in Qolorha-by-Sea, they were abstract.

Dalton then encouraged Twin to make realistic-looking figures so that they would sell better. When Twin went to Johannesburg, no one wanted to buy his realistic carvings and he eventually starved to death. After being told of his son's death, Zim dies, followed shortly by NomaRussia:

> This fuels further anger among the Believers. This unscrupulous woman would not leave Zim alone, they fume. Even when he was called by his wife, she forced her way to accompany him. Now Zim has taken his mistress with him to the world of the ancestors. There is going to be a big war between her and NoEngland (267).

Camagu has to wait for Qukezwa and Heitsi to join him at the cottage until after the *isizathu*, a ceremony for Zim that will take place months after his death. Meanwhile, a surveyor comes to prepare the land for the upcoming developments. But just when it seems that the cause for preservation is lost, Dalton swoops in:

> 'I am afraid there won't be any gambling city, my friend.' Dalton hands [the surveyor] a piece of paper. It is a court order forbidding any surveying of the place. It is accompanied by a letter from the government department of arts, culture, and heritage declaring the place a national heritage site. 'No one is allowed to touch this place!' Dalton shouts triumphantly (269).

Chapter 12 Summary

Post-Apartheid South Africa

Six-year-old Heitsi plays on the sandbank, while "Qukezwa paddles at the shallow end of the lagoon and sings in split–tones" (271). Her song summons the past.

The Middle Generations

The song illustrates how The Man Who Named Ten Rivers conquered the amaXhosa people:

> Pacified homesteads are in ruins. Pacified men register themselves as pacified laborers in the emerging towns. Pacified men in their emaciated thousands. Pacified women remain to tend the soil and build pacified families. When pacified men return, their homesteads have been moved elsewhere, and crammed into tiny pacified villages. Their pacified fields have become rich settler farmlands (272).

Twin knows his brother "died a raving lunatic at the Kaffir Relief House" and that his brother's wife is "the woman of the sea that everyone talks about" (272), but he does nothing to help his sister-in-law and nephew: "There are two big regrets that dominate his life: that his brother died before he could gloat over him, and that he never took the chance to strike out at John Dalton, to avenge his father's head" (272). Twin-Twin has too much to lose. He must leave it up to future generations to avenge his father's death.

Post-Apartheid South Africa

It has been six years since Zim has died, and Bhonco feels that he has lost everything. Bhonco blames Dalton for bringing Camagu to the village and standing with Camagu against progress. Bhonco feels that the only way to set things right "is to see to it that Xikixa's head is restored" (273). He seeks out the businessman, and when he finds Dalton, he says, "Give me the head of Xikixa" (274). Bhonco then hits Dalton in the head with his knobkerrie, a short stick with a knob on top, and then stabs him twice with his *panga* knife:

> Blood spurts out and sprays the walls. Missis runs from her tiny office wailing. Screaming clerks and salespeople join her. Bhonco lashes out at everyone. He is foaming at the mouth as he screeches about the head that has caused him misery. Customers and passersby finally grab him and disarm him. Dalton is unconscious on the floor. He is bleeding profusely from a gaping wound on the head and another one on the arm (275).

The Middle Generations and Post-Apartheid South Africa

In the last couple of pages of the book, the ancestors merge with the people of modern day Qolorha-by-Sea. Not only does Bhonco avenge his ancestor's beheading, but the Qukezwa of the early aughts seems to transition into the Qukezwa of the Middle Generations. Both of their sons are afraid of the sea.

The prophetesses live with Major John Gawler and his wife. They put them on display, before they sail with them to Cape Town and have them "incinerated with a large number of female prisoners and transportees" (276). Nongqawuse's legacy lives on, and a strong tourist trade emerges in Qolorha-by-Sea by people who are interested in the prophesies of the Middle Generations.

Camagu visits Dalton in the hospital. He tells Dalton that Bhonco has been arrested. He goes on to say, "This rivalry of ours is bad. Our feud has lasted for too many years. Five. Almost six. And for what? Nothing!" (277). In response, "Dalton groans his agreement" (277), and the two men make peace.

The book ends with Qukezwa and Heitsi, but it is not clear whether is it the mother and son of the Middle Generations, or the modern Qukezwa and Heitsi:

> Oh, this Heitsi! He is afraid of the sea? How will he carry out the business of saving his people? Qukezwa grabs him by the hand and drags him into the water. He is screaming and kicking wildly. Wild waves come and cover them for a while, then rush back again. Qukezwa laughs excitedly. Heitsi screams even louder, pulling away from her grip, 'No, mama! No! This boy does not belong in the sea! This boy belongs in the man village!' (277).

Chapters 10-12 Analysis

Camagu seems keenly aware of the detriment that feuds and rivalries can bring about. But even though Dalton agrees to put their differences aside, he seems completely unaware of the harm he causes his fellow villagers. He sees himself as their savior, even though he is that foreign, invasive plant that Qukezwa warns the elders about. Even when Dalton is trying to be helpful, his paternalistic, superior attitude causes pain. Zim's son Twin was a talented artist, and it is Dalton that trains Twin out of his own artistic impulses. Dalton teaches Twin to create carvings that are realistic because that is what Dalton values. When Twin leaves for Johannesburg, he is unable to find a market for these types of figurines and is unable to access his own artistic instincts. Although kinder and more well-intentioned, Dalton has the same effect on Twin that The Man Who Named Ten Rivers had on the sons of the amaXhosa chiefs. Dalton unintentionally cuts Twin off from his own generational knowledge and tries to impose his own values and sensibilities.

As the story concludes, the differentiation between the lives of the characters of the Middle Generations and those of modern day Qolorha-by-Sea, become increasingly blurred. Not only do the experiences of the past generation seem to directly affect the actions of the modern-day characters, but we can see how the actions of this new generation are shaping up to affect the generations to come.

Not only will NomaRussia's actions cause a "war" in the Otherworld, but the discontent that she sews in Qukezwa's relationship to Camagu will play out on their descendants. It is not clear that Qukezwa and Heitsi join Camagu at his cottage after Zim's *isizathu*. It is possible that NomaRussia's presence destroyed the connection between the couple.

While the Qukezwas of the world embrace the sea, and the changing times, the Heitsis of the world represent the old ways. Neither is inherently right nor wrong, they just play out differently in different circumstances. Generational forces are met by each individual's personal experiences, and from that something new and unpredictable is created.

The Middle Generations

Xikixa

Xikixa is the father of the twins, Twin-Twin and Twin. He served in the court of King Sarhili. He shared his wealth with his sons and had them circumcised along with the king's son, which gave them good standing in the community. During the Great War of Mlanjeni, Xikixa fought alongside his sons. At one point in the war, the twins, "accompanied by a small band of guerilla fighters—chanced upon a British camp hidden in a gorge" (19). They watch in horror as the British soldiers decapitate the corpse of an umXhosa soldier, and then put the head in a pot of boiling water. Not able to stand it any longer, the guerilla soldiers ambush the camp and are horrified to discover that man that the British soldiers had decapitated was their father, Xikixa. The amaXhosa soldiers capture John Dalton, but British reinforcements run them off before they can take revenge for Xikixa's death and dismemberment. According to his son, Twin, Xikixa's decapitation renders him an ineffective ancestor:

> A good ancestor is one who can be an emissary between the people of the world and the great Qamata. A good ancestor comes between his feuding descendants whenever they sacrifice a beast to him, and brings peace among them. Without a head Xikixa was unable to bring cohesion to his progeny. That was why they were fighting among themselves, and were destined to do so until his headless state was remedied (129).

Twin-Twin

Twin-Twin is:

> [T]he first of the twins to be born, so according to
> custom he was the younger. The older twin is the one
> who is the last to kick the doors of the womb and to
> breathe the air that has already been breathed by the
> younger brother (13).

While they were alike as young men, Twin-Twin and his
brother begin to have divergent beliefs that result in a rift
that continues not only for their rest of their lives but gets
passed down from generation to generation. Twin-Twin
shows himself to be less likely to get swept up in religious
fervor. When the prophet Mlanjeni declares that Twin-
Twin's senior wife is a witch, Twin-Twin objects and is
beaten. The scars from that beating are passed down to the
first-born male of each subsequent generation. When the
prophetesses of the Middle Generations insist that the
amaXhosa have to kill all of their cattle and destroy their
crops in order to bring about the resurrection of their
ancestors and destruction of the white usurpers, Twin-Twin
rejects their claims and refuses to comply. Even though
Twin-Twin has had to make an uneasy alliance with the
British administrators to save his cattle from the Believers,
he resents the British for their actions against the
amaXhosa, including the buying off of the chiefs and the
stealing of land. Twin-Twin rejects the efforts of others to
convert him to Christianity, telling them:

> [H]e could not join a religion that allowed its followers
> to treat people the way the British had treated the
> amaXhosa. He was indeed disillusioned with all
> religions. He therefore invented his own Cult of the

Unbelievers—elevating unbelieving to the heights of a religion (259).

Twin

Twin not only differs from his brother in his ability to get swept up in religious fervor, but also in his ability to love and respect a woman. While Twin-Twin is a rampant womanizer who jokes about raping the young prophetesses with whom he disagrees with, Twin marries Qukezwa, a Khoikhoi woman who had prostituted herself in order to assist the Khoikhoi and amaXhosa soldiers in their fight against the British. While Twin-Twin has many wives, Twin and Qukezwa form a partnership, and Twin often follows her lead when it comes to spiritual and practical matters. While Twin-Twin has the ability to be practical and make uncomfortable alliances, Twin is uncompromising in his beliefs and his actions. Twin-Twin thinks critically and adheres to tradition. Twin is more open-minded and unquestioning of those he chooses to follow. While Qukezwa's concern for keeping their son Heitsi alive eventually leads her to abandon the prophesies, Twin's belief never wavers, and he dies "raving mad" (258) in a facility set up by the British. Twin's legacy is one of conservation for his descendants. They believe in preserving the land where the prophesies were made in the Middle Generations.

Qukezwa

Twin's Khoikhoi wife is treated as an equal by her husband. Twin adopts Qukezwa's religious beliefs and trusts her to lead him and the others to Qolorha when the brothers need to move to keep their cattle from getting the "lungsickness" brought over by European livestock. Like her namesake, she is a spiritual woman who finds herself drawn to the sea.

Prophet Mlanjeni

Also known as "the Man of the River" (14), Mlanjeni was a prophet who blamed witchcraft for the famine that was causing the death of so many amaXhosa people. After Twin-Twin had been beaten because of Mlanjeni declaring that his senior wife was a witch, he felt betrayed when Twin continued to follow Mlanjeni, unquestioningly. But when the British set their sights on arresting Mlanjeni, Twin-Twin stood alongside his brother and the other amaXhosa warriors to protect the prophet, in "the Great War of Mlanjeni" (19). Mlanjeni prophesied that "the guns of the British would shoot hot water instead of bullets" (19), but this did not happen, and the British finally won by burning crops and attacking unarmed amaXhosa women. Mlanjeni died of tuberculosis six months after the amaXhosa forces surrendered to the British. Like Mhlakaza and the prophetesses, Mlanjeni inspires others to take actions that result in large scale death and destruction.

Mhlakaza

The twins had known Mhlakaza when he had gone by the name Wilhelm Goliath. Mhlakaza comes from a distinguished amaXhosa family and his father had served as one of King Sarhili's councillors. Mhlakaza became baptized in the Methodist Church before converting to the Anglican Church:

> Wilhelm Goliath boasted that he was the first umXhosa ever to receive the Anglican Communion. He could recite the Creed, all Ten Commandments in their proper

order, and the Lord's Prayer. He spoke the language of the Dutch people too, as if he was one of them (48).

It is not until he is personally insulted by the treatment he receives from his fellow Anglicans that he returns to his ancestral village, Qolorha. Mhlakaza calls a public meeting to tell everyone that his niece, Nongqawuse, and his sister-in-law, Nombanda, had received prophesies and the amaXhosa must destroy all their cattle and crops. While both brothers initially dismiss the prophesies, Twin eventually becomes a fervent follower.

Prophetess Nongqawuse

While Mhlakaza was the mouthpiece, he reported that it was Nongqawuse and the other young prophetesses who spoke with the "Strangers" (54) who handed down the prophesies concerning the cattle-killing and the necessary destruction of crops. In post-apartheid South Africa, Nongqawuse's legacy is polarizing. While some, like Qukezwa, still believe in the prophesies, there are many who blame the horrors of the Middle Generations on Nongqawuse and the other young women for causing the conditions that allowed the British to gain control over the amaXhosa people.

Sir George Grey

Also known as "The Man Who Named Ten Rivers" (84), Sir George Grey epitomizes colonial aggression. He sees himself as bringing civilization to "the natives": "Of course he had to take their land in return for civilization. Civilization is not cheap" (84). Grey benefits from the divisions within the amaXhosa nation, as well as frictions between different African nations. He is not satisfied with stealing land, but also tries to destroy the culture of the amaXhosa people, as well as the surrounding nations. He renames landmarks, buys off the chiefs, takes over the education of their sons, and replaces their laws. However, Grey sees himself as the benefactor of the amaXhosa people. He considers it in their best interest when he steals their land, tries to destroy their culture, and usurps the authority of the chiefs.

Mjuza

The son of a great prophet, Mjuza has converted to Christianity and supports Grey's colonizing efforts. He argues to Twin-Twin that "Grey was a friend of the amaXhosa [...] Grey believed that all men were equal—well, almost equal—as long as they adopted a civilized mode of dress and decent habits" (85). He also asserted that "Grey was a wonderful man whose only motive for coming to and ruling the land of the amaXhosa was to change the customs of the barbarous natives and introduce them to British civilization" (85). Not only does Mjuza represent those who identify with their colonizers, he also represents the compromising alliances that get formed in times of war or tragedy—Twin-Twin may disagree with Mjuza on the intentions of Sir George Grey, but as fellow unbelievers in the cattle-killing prophesies, he feels he needs to align himself with those who are working on behalf of the British.

Post-Apartheid South Africa

Camagu

Although Camagu does not get introduced until the second chapter, his soul is where the battle for the future of Qolorha-by-Sea, and by extension, where post-apartheid South Africa gets played out.

Camagu had left South Africa in his teen years and had gone on to have illustrious positions at UNESCO and the Food and Agricultural Association. When he returned after what he terms an almost 30-year "exile" in 1994, he found that South Africa had no interest in his expertise in developmental communications. He had been abroad when his country needed him, and he never learned the freedom dance—"the freedom dance that the youth used to dance when people were fighting for liberation" (28).

Camagu has decided to return to "exile," but on the way to the airport, he decides to take a 10-hour detour to Qolorha-by-Sea to find NomaRussia, the young woman who had captivated him with her singing and beauty the night before. In the village, he is unsuccessful in finding NomaRussia, but he soon becomes the physical embodiment of the struggle between the Believers and the Unbelievers. He is an educated stranger amid those that believe in the prophesies of the Middle Generations and those that reject the prophesies and assert that they stand for progress and civilization. Each try to claim Camagu as their own. Camagu finds himself pulled in opposite directions by Xoliswa Ximiya, the beautiful and intellectual daughter of Bhonco, who resurrected the cult of the Unbelievers, and Qukezwa, the wild and spiritual daughter of Zim, the man who leads those who still believe in the prophesies.

Camagu has been displaced because of his exile, but he has the opportunity to find his role in rebuilding his country if he listens and learns, rather than by imposing his own ideas on the people of Qolorha-by-Sea.

Bhonco Ximiya

Bhonco Ximiya, Twin-Twin's direct ancestor, has
resurrected the cult of the Unbelievers. He carries the scars
that were passed down to each first-born son of Twin-
Twin's descendants but does not have a son to pass the
scars along to. While Bhonco considers himself an
"Unbeliever," he actually has very strong beliefs. He is
only an "unbeliever" in relation to the prophesies, but that
does not mean that he is an unbeliever in all things. Bhonco
is very spiritual and engages in rituals that allow him to
time travel back to the mid-1800's and the "sufferings of
the Middle Generations" (3). He also believes strongly in
progress. He spent most of his money educating his
daughter, Xoliswa Ximiya. When it comes to the respect he
has for his wife and daughter, he seems to have more in
common with Twin than his own ancestor, Twin-Twin.
Unlike Xoliswa Ximiya, Bhonco feels connected to his
past. He experiences the pain of his ancestors as his own,
which ultimately results in him avenging Ximiya's
decapitation.

Xoliswa Ximiya

While Bhonco identifies as an "Unbeliever," his daughter,
Xoliswa Ximiya, takes it even further. She rejects the past
entirely. Xoliswa Ximiya does not value tradition or the
past. She is beautiful in a dispassionate way that both
attracts and repels Camagu. When Xoliswa Ximiya inherits
the scars that had previously only been inherited by the
first-born sons of Twin's progeny, the gossip in the village
is that her education, single status, and position of authority
make her more of a man than a woman. In the fight for
Camagu's soul, Xoliswa Ximiya appeals to his intellect but
does not have a visceral effect on him. When Camagu finds
himself aroused with Qukezwa, he purposely thinks of

Xoliswa Ximiya: "Perhaps if he takes his mind off his dire situation, and sends it to dwell on Xoliswa Ximiya's icy beauty, there might be some respite" (152).

Zim

As Twin's direct descendant, Zim is leader of the Believers. The feud between Twin and Twin-Twin is continued by Zim and Bhonco. Both men feel a strong connection to their ancestors, but Zim's sustained belief in the prophesies leads him to value preservation over development. While his concern for sustaining Qolorha-by-Sea's natural state seems authentic, part of it does seem to be fueled by his resentment of Bhonco and the other Unbelievers. If one man takes a stand, the other automatically takes the opposite position. They seem more motivated by their animus for each other than their strong-held beliefs. What began as a sincere difference in opinion by their ancestors has grown into a situation where hate for the other dictates their actions and positions.

Qukezwa

Qukezwa shares more than just a name with her ancestor from the Middle Generations. Both women are spiritual and feel a strong connection to the land. When Camagu hears Qukezwa sing in split-tones, her song captivates him:

Camagu had never heard such singing before. He once read of the amaXhosa mountain women who were good at split-tone singing. He also heard that the only other people in the world who could do this were Tibetan monks. He did not expect that this girl could be the guardian of a dying tradition (152).

While the Qukezwa of the Middle Generations converted her husband to the religion of the Khoikhoi, Zim's daughter leads Camagu to value the prophesies and the history of Qolorha-by-Sea. Both women are comfortable in their own skin and with their sexuality. Qukezwa's apparent immaculate conception of her son also adds a sense of destiny for Qukezwa and Heitsi.

NomaRussia

NomaRussia is the mystery woman who leads Camagu to Qolorha-by-Sea. Although he does not find her until it is too late, she has altered the fate of the other characters by inadvertently luring him to the village. While Xoliswa Ximiya appeals to Camagu's intellect and ego, and Qukezwa appeals to his spirit and sexuality, NomaRussia appeals to his heart. There is a pureness in his feelings towards her that is not present in his feelings toward the other two women. NomaRussia also represents the start of a new rift. She has vowed to haunt the Zim household as payback for the curse put on her by Zim's wife. The negative effects of NomaRussia's vengeance can be seen even before her death. Before Camagu saw her again, all he wanted was Qukezwa and their son, Heitsi, to come live with him. But NomaRussia's return into his life sows discontent and doubt in Camagu's relationship with Qukezwa. It is not clear in the end if Qukezwa ever joins Camagu in his cottage by the sea.

John Dalton

John Dalton's ancestor served as a soldier for the British government and played a role in the beheading of Bhonco's ancestor, Xikixa. While Camagu has an understanding of his outsider status, Dalton seems dismissive of his own. His family's presence in the area for the last five generations gives him a sense of belonging, and he considers the villagers to be "his" people. But rather than living like one of the villagers, Dalton assumes a paternalistic position with his neighbors by managing their finances and choosing which village-wide projects to implement. He resents any mention of his ancestor's role in Xikixa's decapitation, but he lives with the benefits from his great-great-grandfather's plunder of the amaXhosa people. Additionally, he seems unaware that his own actions are sewing resentment and discontent with those around him.

THEMES

Foreign Versus Indigenous People in South Africa

At times, classifying someone or something as foreign is
straight forward, but at other times it is more nuanced. The
first John Dalton who came with the British invaders in the
mid-1800's was clearly foreign. But now that five
generations of Daltons have made their home in Qolorha,
the foreignness of the John Dalton of post-apartheid South
Africa is less clear-cut. At a party of British emigrants who
are planning to leave the country now that the country is
run by a "black-dominated government" (140), Dalton
challenges their connection to the land: "Whenever there is
any problem in this country you threaten to leave. You are
only here for what you can get out of this country" (140).
In turn, the emigrants call out Dalton's own sense of
belonging: "You are not a native, John. You may think you
are, but you are not" (140). To Dalton, the 150 years his
family spent in the country grants him the status of
belonging: "I am staying here [...] I am not joining your
chicken run. This is my land. I belong here. It is the land of
my forefathers" (139). The issue that Dalton tries to avoid
is how it became "his" land, and he does not want to
address the measures his forefathers took to secure the land
nor whomever they displaced.

Camagu's "foreignness" is even more nuanced. He is of the
amaMpondomise clan and spent most of his formative
years in Johannesburg before leaving for the United States.
While he has been shaped by his life in exile, he retains
enough of his formative education to realize that he is a
foreigner in Qolorha-by-Sea. Unlike Dalton, he makes an
effort to be collaborative and take the lead from his fellow
villagers. While Dalton has a patronizing attitude towards
the others, Camagu is open to learning from others and

adapting to their ways. Camagu has spent his whole like adapting, whereas Dalton has never had to make adjustments for others.

Qukezwa realizes the danger of what is foreign. Qukezwa is brought before the elders for destroying wattle and lantana trees. When she explains that it is a foreign tree, Bhonco asks her:

> 'Are you going to cut down trees just because they are foreign trees? [...] Are you going to go out to the forest of Nogqoloza and destroy all the trees there just because they were imported from the land of the white man in the days of our fathers?' (216).

Qukezwa explains the difference between the two types of foreign plants:

> 'The trees in Nogqoloza don't harm anybody, as long as they stay there [...] They are bluegum trees. The trees that I destroyed are as harmful as the inkberry. They are the lantana and wattle trees. They come from other countries [...] from Central America, from Australia [...] to suffocate our trees. They are dangerous trees that need to be destroyed' (216).

It is not necessarily the foreignness of the plants that makes them dangerous, but it's their effects on the indigenous plants. While Camagu's foreignness seems to allow for peaceful coexistence, the foreignness of John Dalton and his ancestors does not.

Conservation Versus Development

The village of Qolorha-by-Sea is divided into two camps, those that support the development of the area into a gambling and water-sports tourist destination and those who want to preserve the integrity of Qolorha-by-Sea by conserving the land and honoring Xhosa culture. The breakdown on who supports development and who does not has a lot to do with how each individual views the past.

Bhonco associates the past with pain and misery, and so he is eager to see the landscape change:

> 'We want to get rid of this bush which is a sign of our uncivilized state. We want developers to come and build the gambling city that will bring money to this community. That will bring modernity to our lives, and will rid us of our redness' (92).

Xoliswa Ximiya not only wants to bring modernity to the village, she wants to destroy the fledging tourist trade that revolves around kwaXhosa's history and the narrative of Nongqawuse:

> Xoliswa Ximiya is not happy that her people are made to act like buffoons for these white tourists. She is miffed that the trails glorify primitive practices. Her people are like monkeys in a zoo, observed with amusement by white foreigners with John Dalton's assistance. But, worst of all, she will never forgive Dalton for taking them to Nongquawuse's Pool, where they drop coins for good luck. She hates Nongqawuse. The mere mention of her name makes her cringe in embarrassment. That episode of the story of her people is a shame and a disgrace (96).

However, Zim and Qukezwa revere the past, and they model their behavior after the Believers of the Middle Generations. Like the other Believers, Zim and Qukezwa take a stand against the planned development. Qukezwa is particularly aware that the "gambling city" (92) will not benefit the villagers, i.e., themselves. The developers will bring in employees from elsewhere, and very little of the money made will be used to benefit the people of Qolorha-by-Sea. The issue not only causes division between Believers and Unbelievers, but also between husband and wife. Now that NoPetticoat has joined the cooperative, she has changed her feelings regarding development: "To Bhonco this is the ultimate betrayal" (234).

Even for the outsiders, their stance toward development is colored by their attitudes toward the past. Camagu feels robbed of his history because his family's move from their ancestral land, and then from South Africa altogether. He longs for a past and is anxious to make roots. His respect for Xhosa history and culture, as well as Nongqawuse and the prophesies, leads him to oppose the development of the village. Because of his work in development communication, he also understands that the money made in Qolorha-by-Sea will not stay in the village. Dalton, on the other hand, has a more complicated relationship with history. He wants to exploit the past, but only the past that benefits him. While he has built his own tourist business around the cattle-killing prophesies of the 1850's he leaves out his own family's part in bringing death and destruction to kwaXhosa.

Withholding Access as a Means of Attaining Power

Whether or not Mhlakaza and the Prophetess Nongqawuse believe in the prophesies, they are able to sustain their followers' belief by making themselves crucial to the realization of the prophesies. Nongqawuse tells the chief, "The new people will come only when you have killed all of your cattle [...] You cannot talk with them now. Only I can talk with them" (80). Mhlakaza, Nongqawuse, and the other prophetesses serve as intermediaries between the new people and their followers:

> The fact that only Nongqawuse, Nombanda, and Mhlakaza could see or speak to the new people enhanced the prestige of the prophets. Many of those who were tempted not to believe were converted by this fact (107).

This also allows Mhlakaza and the prophetesses to instruct their followers with the unquestionable authority of the new people. But when the prophesies repeatedly fail, Mhlakaza finds a way to inoculate himself from blame: "King Sarhili summoned Mhlakaza, who denied he was the source of the prophesies. He put all the blame on Nongqawuse. 'She is the one who talks with the new people,' he said. 'I am merely her mouth'" (131).

Another way that Mhlakaza is able to deflect criticism when the prophesies fail is by continually moving the goal post. When his followers do all that is asked of them and the prophesies fail to materialize, he blames the non-believers. By scapegoating those who do not believe in the prophesies, he turns his followers' attention away from his own failings, and those of the prophetesses, and on to those who had rejected him. In essence, he causes a civil war fueled by his followers' disappointment:

> [Twin and Qukezwa] were angry. But not with the prophets. The Great Disappointment was the fault of Nxito and his spies, who had insulted the new people. It was the fault of all Unbelievers, who had refused to slaughter their cattle and continues to cultivate their lands (211).

The Color Red

Red is the traditional color of the Xhosa, and along with the Thembu and Bomvana, they are known as "the red ones." As a result, "redness" is used as an insult by the proponents of development who view traditional ways as backward and unbecoming: "They want us to remain in our wildness! [...] To remain red all our lives! To stay in the darkness of redness!" (71). When Bhonco confronts Camagu about supporting conservation over development, he shouts, "So I was right. You have chosen your side already. I defended you when the villagers were accusing you of taking the side of redness" (145). When NoPetticoat tells her daughter how much she likes the traditional clothing made by the cooperative, Xoliswa Ximiya responds, "They are the clothes of the amaqaba, mother—of the red people who have not yet seen the light of civilization" (227). However, the color red continues to have special meaning for the Xhosa. Both Zim and Qukezwa decorate themselves with red ochre in honor of their ancestors.

"Redness" signifies the tension between those that would abandon the past in the name of civilization, and those that find value in conserving both tradition and the past.

Water

In its different forms, water runs through the pages of *The Heart of Redness*. The villagers view water as both a powerful and destructive force. Qukezwa is raised to fear the sea: "Her mother, NoEngland, always warned her never to go to the sea alone or with other children" (121). As a result, Qukezwa had not learned to swim:

Once, when she was a student at Qolorha-by-Sea Secondary School, she nearly drowned. She went to the sea with a friend without her mother's permission. She took off her school uniform and tried to swim in her panties. She became stuck between two rocks, and couldn't move an inch. Waves came, buried her, receded, only to come back again. She thought she was going to die (121).

Her friend ran back to the village for help and Qukezwa was saved: "Since her mother's death she has learned how to swim, and has become quite an expert at harvesting the sea. Now she swims with a vengeance and is not scared of the most vicious storms" (121). The water represents the need to adapt to changing circumstances. Just like the Qukezwa of the Middle Generations started harvesting shellfish to survive, this Qukezwa has mastered the elements. At the end of the book, Qukezwa tries to get Heitsi to come into the water with her:

Oh, this Heitsi! He is afraid of the sea. How will he survive without the sea? How will he carry out the business of saving his people? Qukezwa grabs him by the hand and drags him into the water. He is screaming and kicking wildly. Wild waves come and cover them for a while, then rush back again. Qukezwa laughs excitedly. Heitsi screams even louder, pulling away from her grip, 'No, Mama! No! This boy does not belong in the sea! This boy belongs in the man village!' (277).

Survival depends on adaptability, and just like water changes due to its circumstances, Heitsi will have to be open to change in order to lead "his people" (277) into the future.

Snake

Just as the prophesies hold a special meaning for the
Believers, the Majola snake holds an important place for
the amaMpondomise clan. When this type of snake is found
curled up in his bed, he stops it from being killed:

> 'This snake is my totem.' Camagu is beside himself with
> excitement. He has never been visited by Majola, the
> brown mole snake that is the totem of his clan. He has
> heard in stories how the snake visits every newborn
> child; how it sometimes pays a visit to chosen members
> of the clan to give them good fortune. He is the chosen
> one today (98).

But like "redness," there are different reactions to
Camagu's belief in Majola. The men who work for the
hotel speak highly of Camagu:

> [They] talk of Camagu in great awe. They did not expect
> a man with such great education, a man who has lived in
> the lands of the white people for thirty years, to have
> such respect for the customs of his people. He is indeed
> a man worthy of their respect (98-99).

Xoliswa Ximiya, however, is not impressed. When Camagu
disappoints her, she says, "What can we say about a man
who believes in a snake?" (161). While the snake is
something to be revered by Camagu, it is something to be
feared by the maid who uncovered it in his bed. Even
Qukezwa, who values tradition, likens Camagu's
"girlfriend," Xoliswa Ximiya, to a snake.

Clean Versus Unclean

When Mhlakaza first interpreted the prophesies of Nongqawuse, he reiterated her stance that the cattle have been made unclean by witchcraft: "The rapid spread of lungsickness is proving the Strangers right [...] The existing cattle are rotten and unclean. They have been bewitched. They must all be destroyed" (54). This idea of uncleanliness fuels the division between the villagers.

Qukezwa and Twin make the long trek to visit Nonkosi, the newest prophetess, and while there they participate "in the *ukurhuda* rituals where the wonderful prophetess administered sacred enemas and emetic to her followers. They vomited and their stomachs ran all night long" (159). Zim follows the ancestors' lead: "[T]here is no reason why we should not purify our bodies and our souls by purging and vomiting" (166).

To the Believers, the British invaders are punishment to the amaXhosa for turning away from purification and allowing evil to make a foothold in kwaXhosa. The prophesies teach that in order to expel the invaders, the amaXhosa have to gain control of themselves and expel all forms of uncleanliness. The lungsickness spreading through the cattle, and the blighted fields align with this worldview of a need for spiritual rectitude and self-mastery.

1. "Bhonco is different from the other Unbelievers in his family, for Unbelievers are reputed to be such somber people that they do not believe even in those things that can bring happiness to their lives. They spend most of their time moaning about past injustices and bleeding for the world that would have been had the folly of belief not seized the nation a century and a half ago and spun it around until it was in a woozy stupor that is felt to this day." (Chapter 1, Page 3)

   From the first page of the novel, we see that there are fractures even within the realm of the Unbelievers. Even though Bhonco resurrected the cult" (6), he is in conflict with what the expectations are for an Unbeliever. Twin-Twin's rejection of religion in the Middle generations has evolved in the last century and a half, and being an "Unbeliever" now involves more than just a rejection of religion. It also presumes a worldview that precludes the ability to experience joy and appreciate beauty.

2. "The Cult of the Unbelievers began with Twin-Twin. Bhonco Ximiya's ancestor, in the days of the Prophetess Nongqawuse almost one hundred and fifty years ago. The revered Twin-Twin had elevated unbelieving to the heights of religion." (Chapter 1, Page 5)

   It is ironic that Twin-Twin emulates the fervor of the Believers, even as he rejects belief itself. By divorcing ritual from belief, Twin-Twin has retained the form of religion, while abandoning its core function.

3. "Yes, Bhonco carries the scars that were inflicted on his great-grandfather, Twin-Twin, by men who flogged him after he had been identified as a wizard by Prophet Mlanjeni, the Man of the River. Every first boy-child in subsequent generations of Twin-Twin's tree is born with the scars." (Chapter 1, Page 13)

The connection between the generations is not just experienced through memory; it is a shared physical reality. Until Xoliswa Ximiya becomes the first woman to inherit Twin-Twin's scars, each first-born son of each subsequent generation lives the pain of the flagellation received in the name of religion. The pain is not dulled by time but felt afresh by each new recipient.

4. "Twin-Twin's weals opened up and became wounds. After many months the wounds healed and became scars. But occasionally they itched and reminded him of his flagellation. At the time he did not know that his progeny was destined to carry the burden of the scars." (Chapter 1, Page 17)

It is impossible to know what kind of an effect that we will have on future generations. Rachel Yehuda of New York's Mount Sinai Hospital conducted a study of 32 Holocaust survivors and their children and found a higher instance of stress disorders than in Jewish families who did not live in Europe during World War II. The study is evidence of epigenetic inheritance—the idea that environmental factors, including stress, can be inherited. While the study only shows evidence of these environmental factors being passed down one or two generations, each new generation of Twin's line experiences the trauma of the flagellation firsthand, so that it never fades in its potency.

5. "It gnawed the souls of the twins that their father met his end in the boiling cauldrons of the British, and they were never able to give him a decent burial in accordance with the rites and rituals of his people. How would he commune with his fellow ancestors without a head? How would a headless ancestor be able to act as an effective emissary of their pleas to Qamata?" (Chapter 1, Page 21)

    Rather than a complete separation of the physical and the spiritual, the brothers view the body as something that gets passed on into the Otherworld. Later, when the prophetesses speak of the ancestors becoming resurrected, this is also in a physical, rather than just purely spiritual sense. The bodies of the ancestors, as well as the cattle will emerge from the water. Additionally, the decapitation leads to a breakdown in the relationship of descendant and ancestor. By not observing the accepted rites and rituals of burial, the brothers and their descendants have lost a powerful ally in the Otherworld.

6. "He never learned the freedom dance. He was already in exile when it was invented. While it became fashionable at political rallies, he was completing a doctoral degree and working in the communications department of an international development agency in New York. He regrets now that he acquired so much knowledge in the fields of communication and development but never learned the freedom dance." (Chapter 2, Page 28)

    Acquiring the skills that would be valuable in rebuilding South Africa does not make up for Camagu's absence during the heart of the struggle for freedom. The shared experience of fighting from within the country created bonds that exclude Camagu and the other exiles.

7. "The wild fig tree knows all of his secrets. It is his confessional. Under it he finds solace, for it is directly linked to the ancestors—all of Twin's progeny who planted it more than a hundred years ago." (Chapter 3, Page 38)

   Zim does not trace his lineage to Xikixa because he is not only the ancestor of Zim, but he is of Bhonco, as well. His animus toward the Unbelievers even extends toward the father of the twins, and he regards Twin as the founding father of his family.

8. "Hence the anger of her friends. It is that anger of many women of the community shared when they first heard of the scandal. Some blamed both women for trying to damage each other just because of a man. *Ukukrexeza*—having lovers outside marriage—is the way of the world, they say." (Chapter 3, Page 41)

   The affair itself is not what caused the feud between NoEngland and NomaRussia, which had such profound consequences. The feud is a result of each woman turning to the igqirha, in an effort to hurt the other woman. Because NoEngland's curse had such lasting and dire effects on NomaRussia, sympathy is largely with the young woman, even though she tried to steal away her friend's husband.

9. "His daughter has been made principal of the secondary school, so he decided to make a feast to thank those who are in the ground, the ancestors." (Chapter 4, Page 61)

While Xoliswa Ximiya does not honor those that came before her, Bhonco still believes that the ancestors are responsible for her success. While both are a believer in "progress" and "civilization," Xoliswa Ximiya's denial of the ancestors' influence on the outcomes of this world is a radical departure from the Unbelievers that came before her. Even the inheritance of the scars has not made her question her dismissal of the ancestors, as she plans to have the scars surgically removed.

10. "In a slow rhythm the elders begin to dance. It is a painful dance. One can see the pain on their faces as they lift their limbs and stamp them on the ground. They are all wailing now, and mumbling things like people who talk in tongues. But they are not talking in tongues in the way that Christians do. They are going into a trance that takes them back to the past. To the world of the ancestors. Not the Otherworld where the ancestors live today. Not the world that lives parallel to our world. But to this world when it still belonged to them. When they were still people of flesh and blood like the people who walk the world today." (Chapter 4, Page 73)

For Bhonco and the other Unbelievers, it is necessary for them to experience the pain of the Middle Generation firsthand. With their borrowed dance, they travel back to the 1850s to suffer the way that Twin-Twin and his family had suffered. It is what fortifies the feud with Zim and the Believers and is what keeps the past from losing its immediacy. Losing the dance cuts Bhonco and the others from a source of catharsis that ultimately leads to his avenging Xikixa's decapitation.

11. "He embraced the stories that were beginning to spread that Mhlakaza had actually visited the land of the dead—the Otherworld where the ancestors lived—and had been caressed by the shadow of King Hintsa. Even though almost twenty years had passed since King Hintsa had been brutally murdered in 1835 by Governor Sir Benjamin D'Urban, the amaXhosa people still remembered him with love. They had not forgotten how D'Urban had invited the king to a meeting, promising him that he would be safe, only to cut off his ears as souvenirs and ship his head off to Britain. There must be something in Nongqawuse's prophesies if Mhlakaza could be caressed by the shadow of the beloved king." (Chapter 4, Pages 76-77)

Mhlakaza's understanding of history is essential in helping him shape a narrative that will speak directly to the amaXhosa people. D'Urban's betrayal of King Hintsa is still personally felt by those who believe in the prophesies, and the image of Mhlakaza getting the blessing of the murdered king helps bolster his authority among the Believers.

12. "Everyone remembered how the news of Cathcart's death had spread like wildfire, sparking jubilation and impromptu celebrations throughout kwaXhosa. People got to know of the Russians for the first time. Although the British insisted that they were white people like themselves, the amaXhosa knew that it was all a lie. The Russians were a black nation. They were the spirits of the amaXhosa soldiers who had died in the various wars against the British colonists. In fact, those particular Russians who killed Cathcart were the amaXhosa soldiers who had been killed by the British during the War of Mlanjeni." (Chapter 4, Page 82)

"The enemy of my enemy is my friend" is an ancient proverb dating back to the fourth century BCE. Because of the death, destruction and humiliation that Cathcart brought to kwaXhosa, when he is killed in the Battle of Inkerman in the Crimean War by the Russians, the amaXhosa adopt the Russians as their own.

13. "Xoliswa Ximiya is not happy that her people are made to act like buffoons for these white tourists. She is miffed that the trails glorify primitive practices. Her people are like monkeys in a zoo, observed with amusement by white foreigners with John Dalton's assistance, But, worst of all, she will never forgive Dalton for taking them to Nongqawuse's Pool, where they drop coins for good luck. She hates Nongqawuse. The mere mention of her name makes her cringe in embarrassment. That episode of the story of her people is a shame and a disgrace." (Chapter 5, Page 96)

    As dismissive of the ancestors as she is, they have their own kind of stranglehold on Xoliswa Ximiya. She feels that their legacy impinges on the present, and she resents their encroachment into her life, as well as the perception of "her people" by others.

14. "'We stood here with the multitudes,' she says, her voice full of nostalgia. 'Visions appeared in the water. Nongqawuse herself stood here. Across the river the valley was full of ikhamanga. There were reeds too. They are no longer there. Only ikhamanga remains. And a few aloes. Aloes used to cover the whole area. Mist often covers this whole ridge right up to the lagoon where we come from. It was like that too in the days of Nongqawuse. We stood here and saw the wonders. The whole ridge was covered with people who came to see the wonders. Many things have

changed. The reeds are gone. What remains now in that bush over there where Nongqawuse and Nombanda first met the Strangers. The bush. Ityholo-lika-Nongqawuse.'" (Chapter 5, Page 105)

Like Bhonco, Qukezwa experiences the past firsthand. She may not travel back in time, the way the Unbelievers do, but her connection to Nongqawuse and the Believers of the Middle Generations is so strong that she holds their experiences as her own. In this regard, Bhonco is more like Qukezwa than his own daughter.

15. "Most of the refugees in the mountains were the Unbelievers who believed—it was in the days when Unbelievers believed—in Qamata, the god of the amaXhosa. The one who was called Mdalidephu or Mvelingqangi by various prophets of old. Those Unbelievers who believed in Thixo, the god of the white man, were rumored to have been given succor on the grounds of the magistrates' courts, and some as far afield as the Native Hospital in Kingwilliamstown. They were supplied with blankets and food." (Chapter 5, Page 113)

The Unbelievers are defined by their rejection of the prophesies, rather than by their own belief system. Before Twin-Twin disavowed all religion, the Unbelievers continued on with the belief system of their ancestors. But because they did not change course and accept Mhlakaza and the prophetesses, they are now "Unbelievers." That type of framing continues to this day, as well. People are referred to as "non-believers" when they believe in something different than those labeling them. This quote also shows how the need to survive could affect someone's spiritual choices. The

*fact that resources were only shared with those who
converted to Christianity shows how the amaXhosa
people were sometimes pressured to convert by the
British and other converts.*

16. "Bhonco smiles. Then he remembers that as an
    Unbeliever he is not supposed to smile. He is supposed
    to be angry about the folly of belief that started before
    the Middle Generations, and about the sufferings of the
    Middle Generations. And that must be reflected in his
    face. Oh, the burdens that have been placed on his
    kindly disposition by his Cult of the Unbelievers!"
    (Chapter 5, Page 114)

    *Bhonco's natural disposition does not lend itself to
    constant grief, but as leader of the Unbelievers, he feels
    that it is his obligation to continually experience the
    pain of his forbearers. Bhonco has "resurrected the
    cult" (6), and in doing so, he has had to reconstruct
    Twin-Twin's belief system with a 150 years of
    intervening life between the two men. What started out
    as a rejection of belief is now a rejection of everything
    that the Believers hold dear. The Unbelievers have
    become reactionary, and Bhonco rejects joy because he
    considers it to belong to the Believers.*

17. "'I have not joined the Believers. On this issue of the
    gambling city they happen to be on the same side as
    me. The gambling city will destroy this place.'"
    (Chapter 5, Page 116)

    *John Dalton shows that he is not an ideologue. He is
    not loyal to either side and will align himself with those
    he agrees with on any given position. It is this same
    manipulative approach that his great-great-grandfather
    used when simultaneously working for the British*

government, while trying to set himself up as a trader among the amaXhosa.

18. "She walks away. She does not even say good-bye. She just walks away. He looks at her with pitiful eyes. How he longs to lose his breadth in hers. But then, after that had been done, what would they talk about?" (Chapter 5, Page 122)

    Camagu realizes that his desire for Qukezwa is physical, and maybe even spiritual, but it is lacking on an intellectual level. At this point, he still values his western education over what Qukezwa can teach him about his connection to South Africa.

19. "'What is land compared to civilization?' asked Dalton impatiently. 'Land is a small price to pay for a gift that will last you a lifetime [...] that will be enjoyed by your future generations. The gift of British civilization!'" (Chapter 6, Page 123)

    The British justify their theft of kwaXhosa by telling themselves and others that by bringing them Christianity and British culture, the amaXhosa are receiving something more precious than land. The implication is that the amaXhosa are better off as a subjugated people of the British empire than as an autonomous people without the "benefit" of British civilization.

20. "'You see now?' says Dalton to Camagu. 'That's what you get when you dig out the past that is best forgotten.'" (Chapter 7, Page 169)

    Dalton does not have the same relationship with the past that Bhonco, Zim, and Qukezwa do. He is an individualist who thinks that he alone is responsible for his success as a businessman in Qolorha-by-Sea. He does not acknowledge the privileged status he inherited from his ancestors' work with the British invaders, their missionary efforts, and their work in trade. He tries to bury the past while simultaneously benefitting from it. Although they are on opposite sides of the question of development in Qolorha-by-Sea, Dalton is like Xoliswa Ximiya in that he views his life as autonomous from anyone that came before him.

21. "Qukezwa is not convinced. 'All the Khoikhoi are one person,' she says. 'You cannot say the private parts of that woman have nothing to do with me.'" (Chapter 7, Page 170)

    When Camagu tells the story of a Khoikhoi woman whose private parts are kept on display in a Western museum, he does not understand why Zim and Qukezwa get offended. He was educated in an individualist society and has trouble grasping the connection that Qukezwa, who is part Khoikhoi, would feel with this anonymous woman whose body has been desecrated and exploited. To Qukezwa, it is as if the assault happened to her.

22. "When Zim is not dozing under his gigantic tree, listening to the rolling songs of the spotted-backed amahobohobo weaverbirds, he spends hours on the hill, gazing longingly at the place where the sea meets the sky. He knows the Russians will not come. But he waits for them still, in memory of those who waited in vain." (Chapter 8, Page 176)

    Zim has such a strong connection to his ancestors that he is able to put aside the fact that he knows that the

Russians will not come to help the amaXhosa. Toward the end of his life, he honors those that came before him by adopting their mindset that they will be saved, even though he knows it is futile.

23. "Yet Twin and Qukezwa's belief was not weakening. They refused to cultivate their field. Like everyone else, they were hungry. To ease the pain of hunger they tightened leather belts around their stomachs. On days when they could not find any roots, they survived on the bark of mimosa trees. They even had to eat shellfish, which was not regarded as food at all by the amaXhosa." (Chapter 8, Page 184)

Later, Camagu and others make their living off of cultivating the sea. This speaks to adaptability and how the need to survive can change aspects of culture. Shellfish may have been regarded as inedible by those of the Middle Generations, but by Camagu's time, it is considered a delicacy that the best hotels are willing to pay for. Circumstances help shape culture, and the cattle killing and subsequent starvation of the Middle Generations change attitudes towards what is acceptable.

24. "'The advance of Christian civilization will sweep away ancient races. Antique laws and customs will molder into oblivion,' proclaimed the governor." (Chapter 9, Page 206)

The arrogance of Grey shows that there was never an intention of living in peaceful coexistence with the amaXhosa. The intention was always to conquer and replace. Military means were used alongside a legal system that codified the theft of life and liberty by the empire's subjugated peoples.

25. "Camagu regrets ever asking the women to work from home rather than in the room he had allocated for that purpose at his sea cottage. He thought they were being more productive at home. At his cottage MamCirha and NoGiant spent a lot of their time gossiping. Or talking about their cesarean operations. They compared the scars, paying particular attention to their sizes and their shapes. They exclaimed that the scars never really bothered them, even when the weather was bad. 'I often hear people say that when the weather is cloudy or cold the scars itch. I would be lying if I said mine did the same,' NoGiant would say. 'Mine too. It never itches at all. I always forget that it is even there,' MamCirha would respond." (Chapter 9, Pages 218-19)

While much is made of the scars that Twin-Twin and his male descendants suffered, the same kind of respect is not given to the scars that women retain from childbirth. When the women talk about their birthing experiences, they are "gossiping." Scars gotten in fighting and war are valuable, whereas the scars that women receive are something to be dismissed.

ESSAY TOPICS

1. The story is told almost entirely from the male perspective. How does this affect the narrative?

2. How does Dalton deal with his "outsider" status differently than Camagu? How do Dalton's methods escalate the tensions with Bhonco?

3. What effect do you think the reentrance of NomaRussia in Camagu's life has on his relationship with Qukezwa. How do you envision the state of their relationship six years after NomaRussia's death?

4. After so many years of peaceful coexistence, what factors lead to Bhonco taking revenge for his ancestor's decapitation when he does?

5. What qualities did Qukezwa have (and which her husband Twin lacked) that enabled her to adapt after the prophesies failed to materialize?

6. Envision the scene in which NoEngland, NomaRussia, and Zim reunite in the Otherworld. Use textual evidence to describe how these characters might interact.

7. What could Twin or Twin-Twin have done early on to settle their differences before their relationship deteriorated to the point that it did?

8. What effect did Twin's uneasy alliance with the British have on his descendants?

9. Why did Camagu choose to follow NomaRussia to Qolorha-by-Sea instead of leaving for the United States again?

10. How do the British invaders use renaming things to help establish control over the amaXhosa?

Made in the USA
Middletown, DE
19 February 2020